The Last Jews of Kerala

The Last Jews of Kerala

EDNA FERNANDES

Portobello
BOOKS

Published by Portobello Books Ltd 2008

Portobello Books Ltd
Twelve Addison Avenue
Holland Park
London
W11 4QR, UK

A CIP catalogue record is available from the British Library

9 8 7 6 5 4 3 2 1

Hardback ISBN 978 1 84627 098 7

www.portobellobooks.com

Typeset in Sabon and AGaramond by
Avon DataSet Ltd, Bidford on Avon, Warwickshire

Printed in Great Britain

To Felix and Andrew, with love

Contents

Acknowledgements

Thanks to the following people who made this book possible. First, I am fortunate to have publishers who are both inspiring individuals as well as great editors. Thank you to my London publisher, Philip Gwyn Jones, publisher of Portobello Books and Granta, and his team, including Laura Barber and Hannah Marshall. Thank you to Brando Skyhorse and his team at Skyhorse Publishing in New York and to Ravi Singh, publisher at Penguin India in New Delhi. I'm also grateful to freelance editor Daphne Tagg for her insightful copy-editing and to my literary agent Ayesha Karim at Aitken Alexander Associates for her valued support. Thank you to Storm Design for my website: www.ednafernandes.com

The book was made possible by the kind co-operation of the Cochini Jews of Ernakulam, Mattancheri and Israel. Throughout, I have valued their trust and generosity of spirit in the face of adversity, and of course, their stories. I am appreciative of the help I received at the British Museum, the

Paradesi and Chennamangalam synagogues, as well as the Israel Museum in Jerusalem.

Last, love and thanks to my friends and family, particularly: Felix, Andrew Atkinson, Max and Elfina Fernandes, Maria Fernandes, Tania Fernandes, Bernard and Sylvia Atkinson.

Introduction

'Our Days are like Passing Shadows.'

Psalm, 144:4, Inscription on the Paradesi Synagogue
clock tower in Jew Town, Mattancheri

The last of the summer monsoon rains had passed. Bruised
grey skies and merciless sheets of black rain yielded to freshly
washed vistas of blue and green. Coconut palms sashayed in
breezes that blew inland from the Arabian Sea, bearing the
taste of salt and the smell of fish. Jackfruit and papaya trees
shimmered in the sunlight as crows feasted on the fallen fruits,
beaks disgorging seeds and bleeding sweet dark juices into the
soil. As the humidity rose, jewel-like flowers of pink and red
drooped from branches that encircled the stone walls of the
cemetery. Cochin had burst into renewed life.

Skin slick with sweat, the gravediggers completed their
task and gathered up the shovels to withdraw before the
funeral. With their departure, only the parakeets were left to
pay their respects from a vantage point high in the palms

overlooking the old Jewish cemetery, yellow eyes transfixed by the mawkish scene below.

It was September 2006, the burial day for Shalom Cohen, last of the priestly line of *kohanim* in Cochin and one of the dwindling Diaspora tribe known as the White Jews of Kerala. With his death, just twelve remained. An ambulance stopped at the gates of the cemetery, followed by a group of mourners dressed in spotless white. In keeping with Cochini custom, Psalm 91 was sung to relinquish custody of the body to God:

'No disaster shall befall you,
No calamity shall come upon your home.
For He has charged his angels
To guard you wherever you go,
To lift you on their hands
For fear you should strike your foot against a stone.
You shall step on asp and cobra,
You shall tread safely on snake and serpent.'

The last of the White Jews chanted their lamentations as they approached the graveside, hands raised in supplication to indifferent blue skies. Shalom's body had been purified through the cleansing ritual before being dressed in a simple white shroud. Earth from Jerusalem and from Cranganore, the ancient Jewish kingdom of Kerala, was placed in his eyes and mouth. His head was swathed in strips of white linen, his corpse sprinkled with rose water, an old Sephardic custom, and then he was laid in a wooden coffin bereft of all adornment.

The coffin was carried on a palanquin by bearers to the site of the grave, the procession stopping seven times along the way to mark the seven references to the word 'vanity' in *Ecclesiastes*. Wind rushed through the towering palms, their treetops bowed as if in deference. As the parakeets sang their own plaintive tribute, the coffin was lowered into the ground, entombed within the red earth. Once the ceremonials had been completed, the bereaved left the graveside, throwing fistfuls of dust and torn grass over their shoulders to symbolize the tearing of their hearts. The funeral had shaken this tiny community, which is all that remains of a once splendid history that crossed centuries and continents. To those present, it had been a terrible epiphany: with the death of Shalom, the demise of the last Jews of Kerala no longer seemed an event fixed far in the intangible future, but an inevitability, casting its shadow upon them.

*

I came across the Jews of Cochin on my first visit to Kerala in 2002. While working on a story about tea plantations I chanced upon Synagogue Lane, home to a diminishing group of white-skinned Indian Jews who claimed a lineage dating back to the era of Solomon.

Then, as now, they were defensive, introspective and wary of strangers to the point of paranoia. In that first encounter, the White, or Paradesi, Jews claimed they were the only Jewish community remaining in the whole of Kerala as well as the

Jewish community with the oldest history in India. In many ways they were typically Indian, yet they retained an ethnic and cultural identity that was unmistakable. The men and women wore sparkling white lungis and saris, ate Jewish-Indian food and even adapted some of the Hindu customs to their way of life. But they remained orthodox in their Jewish beliefs, and their fair skin was an arresting contrast against the polished ebony complexion of the Keralites. In gleaming garments they wandered through Jew Town like ghosts communing with the living. Back in 2002, the elders still harboured hopes of saving future generations by pressuring the last young Jew and Jewess among them to marry, deploying the most devastating of weapons in their arsenal of persuasion: guilt, on an apocalyptic scale. 'Marry, bear a child. Or the end of thousands of years of Jewish history rests on your heads,' they told the youngsters. The brinkmanship failed and the fate of the White Jews was sealed.

Within the mosaic of histories of the subcontinent, theirs is a story easily overlooked. Yet the fate of the Kerala Jews remained fixed in my mind: a people who vanquished the treacheries of history, fled Israel after the destruction of the beloved Second Temple and later escaped the horrors of the Inquisition in Europe to build a new life in India. Then, when all seemed safe, when they felt assured they were beyond the grasp of extinction, circumstance delivered them to danger once again. What is it like for a people whose end has come?

Imagine if one had been able to witness the end days of the people of Easter Island, the Mayans of Central America,

or others whose civilizations suffered such precipitous down-falls, leaving behind ruined temples as inadequate tributes to what once was. In the book *Collapse: How Societies Choose to Fail or Survive*, Jared Diamond writes of such civilizations, describing how they often wittingly contributed to their disastrous decline and how their evocative ruins continue to mesmerize us:

> We marvel at them when as children we first learn of them through pictures. When we grow up, many of us plan vacations in order to experience them firsthand as tourists. We feel drawn to their often spectacular and haunting beauty and also to the mysteries they pose.

Mysteries such as did they know they were courting destruction, and if so why did they continue to do so? Their ruins are not mere archaeology, but warnings that cry out from the past, symbols of societies that once seemed invincible and yet precipitated their own demise. The ruined synagogues in Cochin, thronging with Nikon-toting tourists, were evidently not grand temples marking a mighty civilization. Yet on a very modest scale, they were the poignant remains of a remarkable and ancient people who dated back to the era of the First Temple, according to their oral history.

They had survived the worst that could be thrown at them – tyranny, dispossession of a nation, the razing of their seat of worship – and yet endured to refashion their community amid the tamarind trees and jasmine blossoms of India. Unlike the

people of the Diaspora elsewhere, the Jews of Kerala were feted, embraced by neighbours of all creeds. While other faiths in India were susceptible to communal violence, the Jews of Kerala remained immune to the troubles that periodically threatened to endanger India's delicately poised religious equilibrium. Part of the reason for this was sheer lack of numbers: they were simply too small a community, too insignificant a lobby to be perceived as a threat to Hindu, Muslim or Christian. They were never a proselytizing people, but cultural chameleons who adapted easily. Over the centuries they proved to be exceptionally adept at surviving the volatile shifts in the political order of the region, from the Cochini royal dynasty to the Portuguese, Dutch and British invading colonial powers.

Despite every advantage, in the end they were undone not by anti-Semitism or war, nor by pestilence or the vagaries of nature, but at the hands of one another as they allowed dissent and rivalry to breed within their ranks. The divide was institutionalized as apartheid between Jews of different skin colour in Kerala, and meant there were ultimately too few marriages, too few children and, therefore, could be no future. When the state of Israel beckoned in 1948, many answered its call and left behind a redundant few.

Today's visitors to Cochin are lured by the romance and longevity of this history and, as they take their snapshots, one can see that the Jews of Kerala have already become a souvenir people. Soon their story will be immortalized also on key-rings and other collectors' items. We have already reached the

epilogue of one of the great stories of the Jewish Diaspora, an epic which will end in Kerala in our lifetime, perhaps within a decade.

For these reasons I went back in the autumn of 2006. I was pregnant with my son at the time, which made me particularly attuned to the sensitivities of a community that had not celebrated a birth in decades. On my return, I discovered that the White Jews were not in fact the only Jewry left in Kerala. There was another equally small community across the waters. The Black, or Malabari, Jews were a distinct group that lived in the main town of Ernakulam and in the nearby villages of Chennamangalam, Mala and Parul, which are all within a few kilometres. They were known as the 'Black' Jews because of their darker skin colour, the same as the indigenous Keralites, which told its own tale of historical integration with the Indians and marriage to converts to Judaism.

The two communities, the Blacks and Whites, had suffered a bitter feud for centuries, their relations marked by apartheid, discrimination, claim and counter-claim over who arrived first in India, who shared common ancestry with the Jewish founding fathers of the subcontinent and who could lay claim to religious purity. In Hindu-dominated India, a country where purity is paramount and bestows ascendancy in the social hierarchy as well as political and economic privilege, these were not petty concerns; they were the cornerstone of survival. The stakes were high and history shows that neither side – Black or White – was willing to relinquish its claims. This lay at the heart of the split within the Jewish community,

evident for the last four centuries, polarizing them when there should have been much more to unite them. It also proved to be their undoing in the end.

Where together they once numbered thousands, with eight synagogues and vast estates of plantations and houses that stretched across the tropical coastal plains of Cochin, today there are fewer than fifty Jews and just one working synagogue remains, with not enough men to form the quorum needed for prayer on Sabbath. The other synagogues have fallen into disuse, crumbling into dust, annexed by jungle and home to writhing nests of cobras.

Their story takes us on a voyage from King Solomon's Israel to modern-day India and back to the Holy Land once more, navigating the great intercontinental migrations and the tragicomic feud of Jew Town which has brought Kerala's Jewry to its knees. At its heart is the battle for racial equality in the backwaters of India, an ancient civil-rights movement that fought segregation in the synagogue, which began in the sixteenth century and succeeded too late to save its people.

It is the end of history for the Jews of Kerala: sixty years after the formation of the state of Israel, sixty years after the birth of the Indian republic, the clock is ticking for India's oldest Jewish Diaspora and it is one minute to midnight.

*

So how did it begin? The available history is a patchwork of folklore, fable and historical fact. The Old Testament indicates

that the first Jews landed on Indian shores thousands of years ago, sailing from Israel on trade missions from the court of King Solomon. Biblical accounts depict sailors and merchants docking at Kerala's main harbour, charged with procuring spices and exotic treasure such as 'elephant's tooth, peacocks and apes'. A further wave of immigrants arrived after the Roman capture of Jerusalem and destruction of the Second Temple in 70 CE, a ruthless act of conquest which sent the Jews into exile, scattering Israel's tribes across the globe like seeds of hope in the wind.

This particular Diaspora never knew persecution in their adopted land. Instead, they were feted by Kerala's rajas as foreign kings, had land, privilege and autonomy lavished upon them. In return for privileges, which included respect for the Sabbath, the right to use symbols of royalty such as parasols and gun salutes, as well as protection from hostile invader forces, the Jews swore fealty to the Cochini rajas, fighting alongside their armies during battles with warring neighbours and acting as advisers at court. They were respected both on the battlefield and in the trading bazaar, seen as valiant soldiers and astute merchants. As the turbaned raja held audiences in his chamber, seated on his silver throne or silk-upholstered day bed as the punkah-wallah gently fanned the regal presence, the Jews were periodically summoned, heads inclined in supplication, to this inner sanctum. The king would receive them in his palace in Mattancheri, which lies adjacent to the Paradesi Synagogue, evidence of the proximity of the Jews to their patron's heart. The land

on which the Paradesi Synagogue and Jew Town was built was provided by the raja, a safe haven when the Jews were driven out from their first city, Cranganore. As a trading people, as people of letters and languages, through the centuries they stayed close to Kerala's kings until India's princely states finally ceded control to the Republic of India at Independence in 1947.

To understand how, after millennia, this once illustrious people has reached its final days, I began at the end of their story, among the remaining White Jews of Synagogue Lane in Mattancheri and the Black Jews of Ernakulam.

Ernakulam, the nearest thing to a big city in the district of Cochin, lies on the mainland's coast and is less than an hour's drive from the southern peninsula of Fort Cochin and Mattancheri. Mattancheri had its own Jew Town once, but today the community is confined to just a cluster of houses on a single street; the rest of the village is inhabited by Christians, Muslims and Hindus who bought up the Jewish homes piecemeal as the Paradesi community emigrated or died out. Separated by a rancorous past and a stretch of swamp-like water that criss-crosses the low-lying land and canals, the Black and White Jews have been compelled to come together in these final days.

This account – a mixture of interview and confession, archive and diary – charts their rise and fall, from the centuries of their glorious heyday to their decline in the twentieth century and the twenty-first-century denouement. Their fortunes were undone by a devastating nexus of apartheid,

inter-breeding, mental illness and the exodus from Kerala after the creation of Israel in 1948.

To some extent this exodus revived the fortunes of the Kerala Jews in Israel and provides a poetic conclusion of sorts for those who chose Israel over India. The majority were sent to live in the Negev. It involved a shocking adjustment, exchanging verdant south India for the barren beauty of the desert; a timeless and orthodox Jewish way of life for a secular and increasingly westernized one; the security and ancient tolerance of Kerala for a life refracted through the deadly prism of the Arab-Israeli conflict.

A few faltered as a result of change, withering once transplanted from their natural setting. Others thrived on the mighty challenge of Zionism, of making the desert of Abraham bloom once more. Akin to some biblical parable, they grew roses and gladioli in the desert and started what was to become a major Israeli industry: horticultural exports. But perhaps, even more miraculous, family life prospered again as Cochini Jews married and raised children. In Israel at least, life has returned for the Kerala Jews.

As thousands made the *aliyah*, deserting one paradise for what they hoped would be another, the Jews left in India have become a people cursed by no marriages, only funerals. They are the old and the unmarried, the embodiment of an exhausted history. The remaining White and Black Jews in Cochin are reconciled to play out the final scene in India.

Among them is Gamy Salem, the sole living descendant of Abraham Barak Salem, a 'Jewish Gandhi' and a contemporary

of both the Mahatma and Jawaharlal Nehru, who eschewed national politics to lead the civil-rights battle for equality in the synagogue and to bring a belated union to the White and Black Jews. Then there is the romantic saga of the young lovers, Balfour and Baby, the first Black and White Jews who defied the elders and married; Sarah Cohen, a widowed White Jewess who is the remaining Kerala heir to the family which once bore the blood of the priestly line, who must now survive the machinations of her Muslim and Christian hangers-on as they plot to inherit her wealth. Babu, the gentle aquarium-keeper tasked with conducting the ritual kosher slaughter of chickens, also has his place as the last *shohet*.

Perhaps the most evocative of all is the plight of the youngest members who cannot, or will not, marry. Anil, a twenty-something Black Jew, longs for 'a Jewish wife who will not give me headache'. Now he must decide – marry outside his people or abandon the land he loves to find a bride. Yaheh is the youngest of the White Jews, who spends her days selling two-rupee tickets to tourists at the synagogue and her nights petting her dog, Baby Doll. For more than a decade, Yaheh and her cousin Keith suffered the pleas of the elders to marry and bear an heir. Steadfastly, they remained apart.

These tragedies went beyond the personal; in another place, another time, the consequences would be theirs alone. But here their decisions blossomed into a communal sorrow. For centuries the Cochini Jews remained segregated, in the synagogue and marital bed. Neighbour against neighbour,

Black against White, exclusive in worship and love. If they had married one another earlier, if the elders had sanctioned love across the boundary, could this have saved them?

Living alongside Jew Town's star-crossed inheritors, celebrating Sabbath and holy festivals with them, witnessing their tears after burying Shalom, the brief burst of joy at a wedding feast for relatives overseas, I saw the life of a people who will soon be consigned to the archives, filed alongside other lost societies who failed to heed the siren of collapse.

As suffocating and draining as the humidity of these coastal plains is the mood of the people: a kind of collective malaise, a brooding fatalism born of the realization that they are the architects of their own downfall. For some of them, all that remains is to endure these final years as a spectacle for tourists in retribution for past sins of discrimination and discord. Privately, they mused, was it their curse or karma?

'We're not a *dying* community. The joke is, we're already dead,' Gamy Salem observed as he distractedly sipped masala chai in his house on Synagogue Lane. 'See how the tourists stare at us, like animals in the zoo, like the living relics we've become. Buy your two-rupee ticket, come see the Jew show while it lasts. This is our ending after two thousand years.'

One

The White Jews of Synagogue Lane

'This land itself was a secret, shared between the sea and mountains, an illegitimate child of the two natural forces, protected by and provided for in a special way. Therefore, there was an assurance of plenty and peace.'

M. G. Narayan, *Cultural Symbiosis in Kerala*

K. J. Joy sat on the steps of the Paradesi Synagogue in Mattancheri and with the gesture of an open palm offered me a seat beside him. If ever a man lived up to his name, it was the *shamash*, or caretaker, of the local synagogue. In his fifties, he possessed still-boyish features and an equanimity that absorbed life's petty trials with easy humour. He was tall, with a languid air and delicately wrought dark features lit by a smile that eclipsed the gloom around us.

He drew his knees up beneath his chin and clasped his arms around his legs in weariness. It had been a long day. Since early morning he had stood on sentry duty outside the sixteenth-century synagogue, shooing away the streams of

tourists who came calling daily. Now as the sun melted into the ragged Mattancheri skyline and the evening settled around our shoulders like a blue-grey shroud, Mr Joy could loosen the tensions of duty and relax.

It was 1 October 2006: Yom Kippur, Day of Atonement and fasting for the Jewish community. The synagogue doors were bolted and the houses of Synagogue Lane were closed to the outside world. Doors and lower windows were shuttered tight, lace curtains at the upper windows drawn, lights off. The heat of the day had yielded to a cool stillness and an uneasy quiet descended. With the approach of nightfall, Synagogue Lane had become a place of repose for phantasmal shadows.

Mr Joy cast a pensive glance down the one-way street that is Synagogue Lane and the heart of Jew Town. Once a bustling community, it was now home to only twelve White Jews.

He had worked as caretaker at the synagogue for twenty-five years, taking responsibility for its daily upkeep, lighting the oil lamps for Shabbat and the festivals, polishing brass work, dusting chandeliers, chaperoning the hordes who came calling every day, corralling groups of excited school kids, explaining the history and generally keeping the public out of the path of the prickly Paradesi elders. Through it all, he remained composed, serene, sometimes a smile of mischievous amusement playing beneath his black moustache.

I pulled out my notebook containing a list of names, the names of the Cochini White Jews I had carefully gleaned from historical accounts and memoirs like jewels from the dust, and began to read them to Joy, who adopted the furtive

manner of a cold war spy betraying classified information to the enemy. His dark eyes darted towards the windows and doorways of the Jewish houses down the length of the street as he answered in a conspiratorial whisper:

'Dead. Dead. This one is also no more.'

'What about him?' I asked, pointing out another name. He nodded in affirmation but then his voice dropped again in apology.

'Alive, but gone to Israel.'

His finger continued down the page, as the roll-call of the dead grew longer until virtually all the names were crossed out and I had begun to wonder if anyone lived.

'Of course, this one stayed,' he said happily, glad to offer some better news at last.

'Yes?' I said, brightening.

'But he died last year. This next fellow – dead. Here, Madamji, also expired, I'm afraid.'

The list of 'Ds' to denote the deceased carried on down the page and overleaf. I started again with a fresh piece of paper, this time writing down a sorrowfully brief cast of those who lived. I showed it to him to confirm.

'Correct. This list is living. But then, I tell you, they're old and they're sick,' he added, as if to caution against too much optimism. It was my first encounter with the community and already their fortunes seemed ill-omened.

'This is worse than I thought, Mr Joy. Who can I talk to?'

'Talk? This is not a good time to talk, madam,' he explained, head wobbling in mild reproach. 'You've come at

the worst possible time. Why, only two weeks ago they buried another of their number. The last of the Cohen men. Shalom Cohen, brother of Sarah, was buried in this cemetery.' He pointed into the distance of Jew Town, which lay ahead. 'Since then, their mood has turned black. After the death of Shalom, they are just twelve. Imagine: to be old, to be the last of your kind, to know your time has come.

*

Cochin lies on the Malabar coast of Kerala, a bounteous state on southern India's western seaboard. Through the ages it has been the scene of commercial trade and shipping and its cultural fusion of Indian, English, Dutch, Portuguese and even Chinese influences is a testament to a turbulent history of invasion first by traders, then by foreign conquerors who battled to control this crucial Eastern spice route.

It was spices, as well as more exotic bounty such as peacocks and apes, that drew King Solomon's merchant seamen to these shores almost three thousand years ago. The connection with Israel and the Jews continued and after the fall of Jerusalem in 70 CE, Kerala was one of the natural safe havens that the Israelites turned to under renewed banishment and persecution.

Their first major settlement was in the ancient trading port of Cranganore, also known as Shingly, which lies twenty kilometres north of modern-day Cochin. But a series of natural and man-made disasters drove the Jews from their

first established kingdom in India and they eventually resettled in Cochin from the fourteenth century onwards.

Kerala is flanked to the east by the densely forested mountains of the Western Ghats, the second highest range in India, which rise to more than 7,000 feet. To the west is the Arabian Sea, the ancient seafaring highway for colonizers and traders. Along this fertile coastal strip merchants came to buy commodities that are still grown for export to this day. It is said these lands once lay underwater until a major seismic force or volcanic eruption elevated the coastal planes to create a utopian landscape.

Today Cochin is not a single place but a district, a cluster of lagoons, islands and inlets which are divided by narrow green waterways. Still waters criss-cross low-lying islands, which are connected to the main bustling town of Ernakulam by bridges as well as ferries that act as taxis to and from the mainland. In the post-monsoon blossoming, flowers erupt in bursts of colour from bushes and trees that overhang the network of natural canals. The dull expanse of water that separates the mainland from the islands is briefly transformed by a thick carpet of pink lotus flowers, as if the gods had cast confetti from the heavens.

Nature's miracle combination of lowlands and a profusion of water have created a lush, tropical belt which yields abundant harvests of coconuts, rice, exotic fruit, spices and seafood, all of which are packaged and sold on throughout India and to markets beyond. Huge container ships from Europe and the Middle East dock in these islands, loading up

goods for export. Cochin is also a major manufacturer of coir matting and palm oil, predominately for the domestic market. At dusk the truck depot comes alive with activity and hollering as battalions of wiry-limbed workers load up huge drums of oil and bundles of coir beneath floodlights before dispatching into the night juddering convoys of gaily painted Tata trucks bearing the motoring legend, 'Horn Please!'

The Malabar coastline has long been a thriving commercial centre. It was in this place that the first merchant Jews made their permanent home. The Black Jews, those of darker complexion and a mixed ethnic lineage after intermarrying with the Indians, are said to date back to Solomon's time and today they are settled on the mainland of Ernakulam. The White Jews, of more recent ancestry mostly dating to the early sixteenth century and hailing from Europe, eventually settled in Mattancheri.

The White Jews were traditionally landowners, businessmen or traders in muslin and perfume from Calcutta, skilled in cask-making and bookbinding, for which they were renowned. In his 1861 memoir, *British and Native Cochin*, Charles Allen Lawson enthused: 'with the most rude tools, they do certainly bind in a style far better adapted to the climate than any one of the brilliantly decorated exteriors of the London publications'.

The Black Jews were also merchant traders as well as artisans: masons, sawyers and carpenters. Among both communities there were a few well-off individuals who acted as money-lenders. By the early nineteenth century Cochin's

position had declined, as Bombay and Calcutta became the pre-eminent trading ports, and most of the Jews of Kerala had sunk into miserable poverty. Today there is little to indicate the glories of the past, when Malabar fuelled the ambitions of explorers like Vasco da Gama and furnished the coffers of European kings.

Mattancheri itself lies just a couple of kilometres from the old historic quarter of Fort Cochin, which today is no more than a fishing harbour, marked by rows of Chinese-style fishing nets like those used by traders from the court of Kublai Khan. At high tide the circular nets are lowered into the water by a winch system operated by three or four workers. The water's surface gives no hint of the fishy treasures that lie beneath. Each day when the nets are raised, a babble of excitement ripples through the harbour as the fishermen reveal glittering hauls of silver sardines, pomfret and grey shrimp as finely translucent as the skin of an old lady's fingers.

Wiry fishermen lever the nets out of the water and retrieve the cargo, which is then dispatched around the region in narrow rowboats that take the fish to market. Local stall-holders buy the best of the stock fresh off the quayside and within minutes freshly fried fish, sometimes plain, sometimes with masala, is served up in newspaper cones to locals and tourists gathered around the local bars and taverns. At night-time, when the stands do brisk business, the smell of fried fish is carried along for a good couple of kilometres if the wind is good. Strings of coloured fairy lights give the dockside a festive atmosphere in the evening, a place to sit, gossip, sip

cold beer and sniff the salt of Cochin's waterfront. Entertainment is provided by the promenade of rich sunburned tourists and elegant Malayalam ladies sashaying in jewel-like saris behind beer-barrel husbands, long white cotton lungis tightly lashed beneath their paunches, stubby fingers carefully brushing their moustaches as they survey the local scene.

Makeshift stalls constructed of bamboo and plaited palm leaves sell tourist trifles such as polished conch shells, hippy beads, tie-dye sarongs to flushed westerners grappling with fists full of rupees. Hawkers sit on stools beside piles of freshly plucked tender green coconuts. Brandishing cut-throat-sharp machetes, the coconut wallahs hack off the heads of the nuts to reveal a sliver of white flesh. Children sit on the kerb-side, tiny hands grasping bulbous coconuts in their laps as they suck the pale milky water through a straw, kohl-rimmed eyes gleaming with delight.

Walk through the streets and you will see a jumble of architectural styles, from the grand Dutch-style villas surrounded by high-walled rose gardens to a Portuguese-built basilica and the old St Francis Church which once held the remains of the explorer Vasco da Gama, who died in Cochin in 1524.

But Cochin is not just a resting place for the relics of old conquerors. It is a living testament to India's ability to absorb its turbulent past into the fabric of a pluralistic society. Here one can listen to the sound of church bells and the haunting cry of the muezzin overlaid with the sonorous lament of the conch shell blown by the high priest at the Hindu temple.

Kerala is a testament to India's religious co-existence, to its traditional ethos of tolerance, despite the periodic eruption of religious extremism that scars India's long history. Here in Cochin the Keralites have shown that Hindu and Christian, Muslim and Jew can retain a distinct religious identity and yet live in harmony. The Jews enjoyed a harmony that is rare in their history, living in peaceable accord with neighbours of every faith. Ironically the only discord they experienced was from within, the worst discrimination and humiliation they endured was at the hands of their fellow-Jews.

With these thoughts, I approached Mattancheri's Jew Town the day after Yom Kippur. Synagogue Lane had sprung into life again as the local tourist shops got ready for the stream of visitors. In the distance I could see one or two of the White Jews, dressed in the traditional Malayalam cotton lungi, distinctive because of their pallor. I looked up at the row of plastered stone houses, Jewish homes, many now empty or rented by the Kashmiri or Christian traders. Examining the rather austere architecture, my eye was drawn to the intricate metalwork that covered the upper-storey windows of the first few houses. On one house the window grilles portrayed the Star of David, painted in the same cornflower blue as the Israeli flag, the resplendent blue of brilliant summer skies over Jerusalem. On the next house was the ancient Sanskrit symbol of the Swastika, for thousands of years the Hindu symbol of well-being before it was hijacked and adulterated by the Nazis. On a third house was the crescent moon of Islam, picked out in green and white.

A Star of David, a Hindu Swastika and a Crescent of Islam all residing on Synagogue Lane. With a charge of excitement, I headed towards the synagogue, next to the local police station and a bookshop run by a Christian family. The Paradesi place of worship is a simple, whitewashed rectangular building, with an attached clock tower that has four faces: one face has an inscription in Hebrew, another in Malayalam and a third in English. It was built in 1568 by the leaders of the White Jewish community. The Paradesis, the Malayalam word for 'foreigners', were wealthy European Jews who fled the Inquisition in Europe to settle in India and rebuild their lives. Some of these European Jews intermarried with the older Jewish communities which had been long settled in the region, having come to Cochin from Cranganore after the great flood of the River Periyar in 1341 silted up the harbour there. But the majority of the Paradesis remained distinct, marrying their own.

The Paradesi Synagogue is not the first to have been built in Kerala – there are synagogues with far older foundations – nor is it the most beautiful. But certainly it is the most famous and it remains the oldest working synagogue in India. It is the only synagogue of the Cochini Jews which still holds religious services, albeit rarely, and it undoubtedly has a charm that casts its spell on all who visit. It is this synagogue more than any other that put the Kerala Jews on the map, not just in India but worldwide, a cross between a museum and a place of pilgrimage. Non-Jews come to learn of the amazing history. Jews come to pay tribute to one of the oldest of the Jewish Diaspora communities.

Inside a young woman with curly short hair and huge dark eyes engulfing a slender face sat at a wooden table with a small metal cash box set before her. She was in her mid-thirties, yet her expression was weary, as if the burdens of an empire were bearing down upon her spare frame. And in some ways they were.

Her name was Yaheh Hallegua, daughter of Johnny and Juliette Hallegua, the sister of Sammy the synagogue warden. She had the familiar look of the Synagogue Lane women: wan complexion, long, drawn-out features, fleshy lips and a high forehead. Yaheh held a special place in the community: she was the only woman of marriageable and child-bearing age. The only bachelors were her cousins Keith and his brother Len. For more than a decade the elders had tried to force her to marry and bear a child to continue the Paradesi line. By refusing, she extinguished their prayer for a reprieve.

Yaheh now spent her days at the synagogue selling tickets to visitors for two rupees a time, periodically shrilling instructions to cover their bare shoulders, or brusquely turning away those who disrespectfully wore above-the-knee skirts or shorts. She burned on a short fuse, bored and irritated by the absence of variety in her years of responsibility as mistress of the gate, in charge of the endless cavalcade of tourists who all asked the same things and wore the same inappropriate dress. She retreated from the tedium by closing herself off to all around her, like a house with its shutters bolted tight to hide all signs of light and life inside. The grinding repetition of life was only part of her story. I was to learn later of her warmth

and enjoy a smile that was as spectacular as it was unexpected.
However, on that first day the expression was sour, the tone
taciturn, the conversation cold to the point of inflicting verbal
frostbite, and it was with great relief that I saw Joy standing
in the small courtyard outside the main synagogue itself. Mr
Sunshine was giving the tourists the synagogue spiel, telling
the story with the contagious enthusiasm of a father reading
bedtime stories to his children. I slipped off my shoes and
went to join him.

The old synagogue is typical of the Jewish Cochini style:
rectangular, with a narrow staircase to the right of the entrance
leading to an upper gallery where the women once sat in
purdah behind latticework screens. At the front of the central
hall is the Ark, a wooden box or cupboard which houses the
seven copies of the sacred Torah scrolls, hidden from view
behind a silk hanging. Each of the ancient scrolls is contained
within a cylindrical wooden casket covered with sheets of
beaten silver. On top of each casket is a solid gold crown,
studded with rubies, sapphires and emeralds, one of them
donated by the Maharajah of Cochin in 1803. In front of the
Ark is the tevah, a reading lectern on a small platform from
which the Torah is read during services. Narrow wooden
benches are arranged in a horseshoe shape around the edge of
the synagogue, flanking the Ark on three sides. Light floods in
from huge open-shuttered windows and broad dust-filled
sunbeams criss-cross the blue and white tiled floor.

The cool plastered walls are festooned with a rainbow of
silk wall hangings, red, orange, purple, blue and shimmering

gold, which reflect the daylight. From the whitewashed, wooden-beamed ceiling hang myriad Venetian and Belgian crystal chandeliers and lanterns: a mismatch of different sizes, shapes and colours that lend an air of baroque opulence to this otherwise simple room. These days the lamps are rarely lit to display their full glory, for coconut oil to light the lanterns is expensive, and who would be there to see it apart from a handful of old-timers? But on special occasions, such as the festival of Shmini, it remains the special duty of Mr Joy to light the lanterns, to restore the synagogue to its full majesty. With diligent reverence the old Roman Catholic caretaker would mount his wooden stepladder and each chandelier would be carefully lowered, its crystal drops meticulously dusted, compartments filled with sweet-smelling coconut oil and then lit with a taper before being hoisted back into place. The most important lamp of all and the only one kept burning at all times is the *ner tamid* or 'eternal light', suspended by a chain from the ceiling directly in front of the Ark. Those privileged enough to witness the Paradesi Synagogue in its fully lit splendour can never dispel the vision: one of ethereal brilliance, as if a tiny corner of heaven had fallen to earth for those few hours.

The floor of the synagogue is paved with hand-painted Chinese willow-pattern tiles which were brought to Cochin in 1762. The tiles, each one bearing a unique design, were originally destined for the Hindu temple of the maharajah, but there are various legends about how the tiles ended up adorning the Paradesi Synagogue. Gathering his audience

around, Mr Joy crouched low on the ground, fingertips splayed like a black starfish on the cool tiled floor as he gazed up at the circle of faces with shining eyes. Clearly the story of how the Jews secured the precious tiles was one of his favourites.

'See how the story of these tiles tells of the cunning of the Paradesi Jews,' he began. 'One of the Jewish leaders saw the tiles that had been ordered by the raja. These were special tiles, each one different, each telling a new story, each hand-painted and sent in a special royal shipment from China. This one clever Jew saw the beauty of the tiles and wanted them for his synagogue. But how to persuade the raja not to use them in his temple? This was the problem. So he told the king that the tiles were made using an ingredient that included the blood of a cow.' He chuckled in delight at the audaciousness of such a scheme.

The story is recounted in the memoirs of Shlomo Reinman from Galicia, who came to Cochin and settled there in the 1840s after marrying a local Jewess. His writings tell of the king's horrified reaction when informed that tiles purchased for his sacred temple might be polluted with the blood of the sacred cow. 'To think that he should tread upon a floor in which the blood of the cow he worshipped was killed and then mixed,' said Shlomo's account. The tiles were duly rejected and given to the neighbouring synagogue for its own use and to this day they remain one of the most remarkable features of the building.

Down the ages the Jews gathered eye-catching treasures

from around the world to furnish their beloved place of worship: chandeliers from Venice, tiles from China, sumptuous silks from Benares and the 'Haile Selassie Carpet', a gift from the former Ethiopian President. The carpet is unrolled before the Ark on only the most auspicious occasions. Haile Selassie, known as the Lion of Judah, visited the synagogue during his period of rule. When the rolled-up carpet was delivered to the synagogue it triggered a security fracas as local police chiefs feared it harboured hidden explosives and insisted on their men supervising the unpacking and unfurling of the carpet before clearing it for use.

The Lion of Judah is just one of the great and the good who came to pay tribute to this modest synagogue. To this day, generous visiting benefactors, both Jewish and non-Jewish, give donations to the synagogue to help finance its upkeep. For it could scarcely survive without their charity or the patronage of the powerful. Its visitors' book includes the signatures of Jawarhalal Nehru, Indira Gandhi, Lord Mountbatten and the Dalai Lama, among others.

And it has always been so. The White Jews were always a magnet for important visitors to Kerala. Even before the age of mass communication, their story fired the souls of intellectuals, travellers and the faithful who came to see this anthropological marvel: a Jewish community who were as white as they were Indian. Numerous chronicles describe what they looked like, how they lived and indeed the feud that existed with their black brethren across the waters. All outsiders noted the clear distinction that existed between the

White and the Black Jews of Cochin, but because of their unusual appearance and their facility with European languages,
the focus was always on the White Jews. Charles Allen Lawson
gave an eyewitness account in his memoirs:

> The Cochin Jews are divided into two distinct classes,
> one known as the... White, the other as the Black Jews.
> The former are the descendants of the first settlers by
> marriage solely with one another. Their complexion is
> not exactly European, but it is the pale olive freshness
> most allied to it and the delicate carnation of the tips of
> the fingers proves that no native blood flows in their
> veins. The features are fine if not noble; broad and high
> forehead, roman nose, thick lips, generally concealed
> by a most luxuriant, jet-black curly beard.

His description of the women was less flattering and somewhat
lacking in chivalry: 'Whilst the Jew seems to improve in
appearance as years creep on, the Jewess "fades as the leaf
fades", and at thirty years of age is plainness itself.' The
children were described as 'leprously white'.

Other accounts show how visitors were intrigued by this
insular people and their culture so alien to the backwaters of
India: 'Jews, nothing but Jews, a pallid Jewry whose blood
has been impoverished by the stifling houses and the Indian
climate contrary to all recognized theory,' wrote Pierre Loti in
his 1903 travelogue, *India*. Loti, a pseudonym used by French
captain Louis Marie Julien Viand, observed:

... two thousand years of residence in Malabar have
not in any way modified [the] Jewish faces. They are
the same people, dressed in the same long robes that
one meets at Jerusalem or at Tiberius; young women
with delicate features, old wretches with hooked
noses, children with pink and white complexions who
wear paper curls over each ear just as their brothers
do in Canaan.

Then as now, visitors were drawn to Synagogue Lane to
marvel at the survival of this foreign clan, fascinated by their
ability to survive in India alongside the locals, to thrive and
establish their own businesses, whilst retaining an unmistakable purity of lineage. Yet one commentator after another
sensed a fatalism that ran through the Paradesis like intricate
veins of black through white marble, and recognized the
foreboding that prevailed over Jew Town. As Loti noted:

The decaying sadness and walled-in isolation of this
town seemed to assort ill with its setting of sky and
palms; after taking this sudden turning one is no
longer in India and the mind becomes bewildered, and
we no longer know where we are; perhaps in the
corner of a Leyden or Amsterdam ghetto that has been
transported to a land whose tropical sun has baked
and cleft its walls.

The writer rightly described the architecture of Synagogue
Lane as Dutch-style: tall, densely packed terraced stone houses
with narrow windows that were not well suited to Kerala's

stifling tropical climate. Reading his journal, I sensed that Loti felt almost claustrophobic in Jew Town. Here in the heart of India, integrated and respected even, the Jews still remained apart, distinct, a refugee people. For the Jews, Kerala was always meant to be no more than an interim homeland, a sanctuary until they could return to the land of their fore-fathers, ending their spiritual dislocation.

In the past, a yearning for their homeland may have been the cause of the Jews' melancholy. But by the new millennium, many of them had returned home, to Israel, leaving the few who remained to languish in a new sadness: ironically, a realization that soon their community would be lost to India for ever.

The First Couple of Mattancheri's remaining White Jews was the synagogue warden Sammy and his wife Queenie, daughter of the late Sattu Koder, wealthy businessman and Jewish patriarch. Their children had left long ago for America and the couple now lived alone in a grand house, cared for by a retinue of servants. A few doors down lived Johnny and his wife Juliette. Johnny also helped run the synagogue, dealing with its upkeep and administration, and his younger daughter Yaheh lived with them. Yaheh's beautiful older sister had left long ago to marry and settle in Israel, where she lived with her husband and three children. 'All boys,' her mother joyfully told me.

Blossom Hallegua lived towards the top of the lane with her sons Keith and Len. Blossom was now in poor health, bedridden and reliant upon her sons for survival. Blossom's

boys were the last eligible 'young men' left in Synagogue Lane, in their late thirties and forties, and both had resisted efforts to marry them off. Keith had once been a promising local businessman, running his own travel firm which catered to tourists, but since coming into family money he had retreated more and more from public view and now he was a virtual recluse. During my entire stay I never once saw him or his brother. Locals living on the street told me that Keith would lock himself away for days on end. He never came to synagogue, he never went to parties and he rarely went out. 'There was a time when we used to sit, gossip, he was fun. But lately, he's not been... the same. There's something that's not quite right,' said one of his neighbours, *sotto voce*.

Isaac Ashkenazy was another bachelor, now in his ninth decade, but without the Byronesque brooding of his younger neighbours. Isaac was joyful in his solitude. He had never married, resisting all efforts with a violent passion, and he continued to live alone in the old family house called Sassoon Hall. He was an elusive figure, of thoughtful disposition, always dressed in immaculate white kurta pyjama. Isaac was also the image of Alfred Hitchcock, and in true Hitchcock style would make dramatic, fleeting appearances when least expected, head turning slightly to fix his audience with large, baleful eyes for a split second before slipping into the shadows of his grand mansion. There was no point knocking on the door, tapping at windows, telephoning even: he refused to be drawn out. When we finally met at a party, he turned out to be adorable company: funny and with a rather giddy sense of

humour, giggling like a saucy schoolboy about the need to avoid marriage and predatory women at all costs. 'Especially at my age,' as he put it.

Isaac's neighbour was Sarah Cohen and her neighbours on the other side were the Salems. Gamy Salem was a Black Jew who had married Reema, a Paradesi. They were Jew Town's only 'mixed' couple.

These were the last twelve, including Gamy, who had honorary 'White' status through marriage. I was yet to meet the Black Jews across the waters, a community which had a completely different dynamic: younger, more integrated and, curiously, happier and more reconciled to their shared fate of extinction.

How was it that this became their shared destiny? There was no plague on their houses, no war, nor famine. While other Diaspora communities had thrived through adversity, the Cochini Jews had lived in an earthly paradise. In the end, death came not at the hands of others, but one another. The question was why? The elders, keepers of history, were as good a place as any to start looking for the answer.

Two

King of the Indian Jews

'I travelled from Spain.
I heard of the city of Shingly.
I longed to see an Israeli King.
Him, I saw with my own eyes.'

Rabbi Nissim, fourteenth-century poet and traveller

Within days of my arrival, I had become a stalker of the Jews of Synagogue Lane. I invaded their 'natural habitat', lurking amidst the camouflage of the Kashmiri shops while I scanned the horizon for their distinctive markings: white skin and silver heads encased in *kippah* caps. Once I spotted my prey, I homed in silently, without pity.

I began by targeting the biggest beast among them: synagogue warden Sammy, the man with all the answers, I was told. It proved to be a risky endeavour as in the end I would be the one who eventually received a mauling from the aged community patriarch.

Sammy was an elusive and mercurial character. Some

spoke of him as a prickly yet kindly man, a grandee who came from one of the oldest families of White Jews, who had married the richest Jewess in town, thereby cementing his position in the pantheon of elders. His detractors deemed him proud, arrogant, prone to outbursts of anger, a man privately tormented by the realization that the Paradesi Synagogue would be closed at the end of his lifetime, on his watch. Sammy lived with the knowledge that he would go down in history as the last warden of the last working synagogue in Kerala. His was the inevitable legacy of failure.

He was not the easiest man to like. But it was easier to understand the source of his volatile moods. Every time a stranger visited, every time he explained the story of his people, an unspoken question hung in the air: why did it end? Behind the decorous glory of the synagogue and a history that stretched like a golden pathway back to their Jerusalem, there was the realization that the road lying ahead was a wasteland stripped of the hope that only youth can bring to an exhausted generation. The others had the luxury of hiding behind their lace-draped windows, screening out reality if they wished, but Sammy was the man in the public eye who dealt with that question every day.

The pressure upon him was particularly intense at this time of year, the height of the festival season. I had landed on the day of Yom Kippur, the day of abstinence and reconciliation which had seen this small community pray and fast for almost 24 hours. The timing was not deliberate, but it proved far from ideal, as the community was stretched – emotionally

and physically. Despite most of them being in their seventies or eighties, they had prayed inside the synagogue for hours on end, much of it standing, taking no food or water from daybreak to sundown.

As I waited outside Sammy's house, chatting to the Kashmiri family who ran the emporium opposite the Hallegua home, word had reached the warden that a stranger was in town who was asking about the history of the Jews of Cochin. A servant emerged from the Hallegua house and crossed the lane to speak to me: 'The Master wishes to know what you want.' As I explained, he listened avidly, head wobbling from side to side in careful appreciation, and then scuttled through the brown shuttered doors to report back. At the upstairs windows of the Hallegua house, the curtains fluttered and one could discern the shadow of someone looking out on to the street. I sat on a stool and waited, my only source of amusement being the ambling promenade of tourists who ran the gauntlet of the Kashmiri merchants.

A while later Sammy emerged, a gaunt figure in white kurta pyjama, accompanied by his wife Queenie, who followed on behind. Queenie lived up to her aristocratic reputation, blessed with an imperial bearing and melodramatic glamour that seemed out of place amidst the provincial goings-on of Cochin. Like a Picasso masterpiece-made-flesh, she made her way towards the car, her mouth a gash of lipstick red against a white, meticulously powdered face, her hair carefully coiffed into a halo of curls around a domed forehead. The two were

on their way to a shopping expedition and their driver was polishing the white Ambassador car in anticipation of their departure. He then stood to attention by the back door, holding it open for them. With a look of regal curiosity, as if examining a new species of insect under a microscope, Queenie gave me the once over before sweeping into the back of the car, uttering not a word.

An audience of local Keralites and Kashmiris had gathered by now to witness the encounter with Sammy, who came over to speak to me. His face was a mask of small, hard features, any emotion disguised beneath a veneer of hauteur. His light eyes were clouded over with milky cataracts, his mouth a tight little line, complexion blanched under the noon sun, with blue veins prominent at his temples. I extended my hand and took his: the palm felt dry and papery, with neither warmth nor welcome in its touch.

'You're seeking information on the Jews of Cochin,' he said, aware of the people gathered around us, keen to play to the gallery. 'What do you wish to know?'

'I'm looking for some guidance on the history.'

'I've no time for guidance. Every day we're besieged by people like you: journalists, writers, tourists. They come knowing nothing, nothing of our history, thinking I've time to do nothing but talk.'

'I know you're a busy man,' I began, feeling less like the predator and more like a child protesting to the headmaster.

'Then write your list of questions, leave them at my house

and I'll make an appointment for you on Wednesday or Thursday, before the festivals begin again.'

No pleasantries, no chit-chat. With that he left, stooping to join his wife in the back seat before being driven into town, the wheels of the Ambassador leaving the rest of us engulfed in a puff of grey dust as the car peeled off.

The audience of Kashmiri storekeepers, servants and hangers-on broke into animated conversation, congratulating me on crossing the first hurdle. 'Now all you have to do is get him to keep his promise,' added one. 'Maybe he will, or maybe he won't.' A few doors down I could see Gamy Salem standing in his doorway, looking on with a wry smile. Something about that smile set off an alarm bell in my head.

That same day I dropped off my list of questions with details of where I was staying. The servant opened the door of the Hallegua residence and accepted the piece of paper with lowered eyes and open palms, as if receiving an ambassadorial missive. 'Thanking you, madam. The master shall see it.'

Days passed. Tuesday came. Wednesday came, then Thursday. Tomorrow would be Friday, the beginning of a period of festivals which would go on for a couple of weeks. The Sabbath deadline was looming, so with rising anxiety, I paid another visit to the warden's house. I was in luck. Sammy was conversing with one of the neighbours outside. He finished his conversation and approached with a spark of malevolent delight in his eyes.

'Your questions are no good,' he announced in a booming

voice that ensured everyone heard. 'I don't have time to answer your questions.' Was this a genuine 'no' or the usual Indian prelude to negotiations? I cast my mind back to my list.

'You've chosen to ask questions about the history of the Black and White Jews. We don't wish to discuss the past. That history is finished.'

'Perhaps it'd be helpful to hear your side.'

'We are the first. What else to say? I don't care what the history books claim. I've no time for questions. I've no time for interviews.'

'What about next week?' I responded. 'I've come especially from London to meet you.'

'Then you've wasted your journey, madam.'

A look of triumph flitted across his face as he shoved the piece of paper back into my hands, turned and went into his house. Throughout the exchange, Gamy was standing on his threshold observing the scene, his face a picture of wry amusement still, as if to say, 'I could have told you this was coming.'

The exchange had been the nearest thing to drama that Jew Town had seen in weeks. It was amusing: the foreigner spending her days stalking the cantankerous Paradesi warden. Who would break first? After watching in silence, the traders and hangers-on broke into renewed chatter, a cacophony of Malayalam, Kashmiri and Hindi as they gathered around in a conspiratorial huddle. Hands gesticulating as if swatting flies above their heads, they expressed

particular outrage that I should be addressed so brusquely while pregnant.

'Sit down, come into the shade, take water. To speak to a pregnant woman like this! They say he's arrogant and now you see it yourself,' said one of the shopkeepers, offering me a stool next to a basket of bronze Ganeshes, the Hindu god for removal of obstacles. The Kashmiri, ever the wily salesman, quietly advised that the purchase of a Ganesh might prove fortuitous.

'Now you're seeing the nature of this man. This isn't the first time, I'm telling you,' added another. 'Arre, Gamy. Tell her.'

Gamy wobbled his head, a typically ambivalent Indian gesture for tricky situations that could be taken any number of ways: yes, no, possibly, or no comment. I showed Gamy my list of questions. He sucked his long yellowed teeth and then with great deliberation untied and retied his lungi extra tight below his small round stomach, as if preparing to deliver a devastating verdict.

'See. This question here,' he pointed halfway down the page. 'You mention innocently, "What is the historical relationship between the Black and White Jews?" Then you mention in passing the great ancestor of the Cochini Jews, Joseph Rabban,' said Gamy, head now bobbling excitedly as he tapped away at the list. 'See. The problem is not that you know too little of our history. The problem is you know too much. Our Sammy doesn't want people to know the truth. That the White Jews persecuted the Blacks. That there was

apartheid. That the great forefather Joseph Rabban was a Black Jew, not a White. If you had come knowing nothing, you'd have your interview by now. You'd be welcomed with open arms. Then Sammy could tell it the way he wanted. He knows you know the real story. That, madam, is your problem.'

According to Gamy, Sammy was not just the warden of the synagogue but the guardian of its legacy, charged with preserving what remained: a wonderful story of endurance. As I sat amid the raffia baskets, the pregnancy hormones were raging. I decided I would bide my time, calm myself and then return to the synagogue the next day to try again. Surely even the notorious Sammy Hallegua could not say no to a pregnant woman inside the synagogue just hours before the Sabbath?

The next day, I readied myself to meet Sammy on his own territory. It was approaching eleven o'clock and already the humidity had left man and beast listless. The neighbourhood crows hunched in the trees in a sun-drunken stupor like old men suffering from hangovers. The street was quiet. Most of the residents were holed up inside, legs resting on their planters' chairs as they sipped nimbu panni and iced lassi beneath softly whirring ceiling fans. Cotton bed sheets hung from the open doorways to block out the fierce light, periodically catching a breath of breeze and fluttering up towards the sky like white-gloved hands waving their good-byes. The Kashmiris, used to the pine-cool climes of the Himalayas, were the only ones who stood by their trading posts, wilting by the roadside as they lifted rosewater-soaked

handkerchiefs to cool their brows. In the local police station
next door to the synagogue, the sole sign of life was the khaki-
clad duty officer spreadeagled in a chair near the door, danda
skew-whiff as he snored in happy oblivion, with a litter of
pups fast asleep at his feet.

When I entered the synagogue antechamber, Yaheh
avoided eye contact as I paid my two rupees. Clearly, the
word on the street was that Sammy had no intention of
helping and I feared the community would now close ranks
on me before I had even started. I slipped off my shoes and
went into the main chamber.

The synagogue was empty save for Joy doing some light
dusting, and Sammy holding court with a couple of foreign
tourists clad in shorts, T-shirts and wraparound sunglasses.
He was a different man from the one I'd met earlier: his eyes
were animated and his countenance bright. He was regaling
his audience with the story of how the White Jews were the
original settlers in Cochin. I joined the group and listened in.

'Are there any books for sale?' asked one man with an
American accent, reaching for the wallet in his back pocket.

'There're no books, I'm afraid. But you can buy postcards
just outside,' Sammy replied amiably.

As the Americans prepared to leave, I again broached the
subject of speaking with Sammy. But the impending Sabbath
had not induced a new mood of benevolence after all. Sammy
exploded in fury. His face turned puce and his arms flailed
like the tentacles of a disturbed squid.

'We have no need for any book on our history,' he

screamed. 'We had two professors live with us for one year. We helped them, we told them the truth and what did they write? Errors and lies.'

'What lies?'

'I have no time for you people. You can go to hell,' he said, and began to walk away. 'I don't give a damn,' he yelled. 'This is my synagogue. Mine. And I will do what I wish with it. I can close the doors to all visitors. I can ban everyone if this is my wish and they can go to hell if they don't like it.'

He stormed out of the building with sweeping strides, leaving us to digest the outburst in a silence broken only by the mocking chirruping of the parakeet outside. Within the hour, word had spread through the street about how Sammy had raged at a pregnant woman inside the synagogue. The bookseller Godfrey had told the neighbouring Kashmiri shopkeeper, who told the antiques emporium manager, who told the next store and the next, until the story reached the other Jews living on the street. Only the sleeping policeman missed out on the drama. My worry now was that the White Jews would freeze me out, following the example of their leader. Instead, as news of the synagogue stand-off spread, it brought out the best in the Paradesis. Even Isaac Ashkenazy, the resident Hitchcock look-alike, paused to give a fleeting glance of sorrowful condolence before vanishing like a zephyr into the shadows. As I walked past the Kashmiri shops, the stallholders paused to commiserate. 'Don't mind,' said one. 'He's like this. Sometimes he just goes crazy.'

As I passed Gamy Salem's house, the old cynic stood in his doorway watching. The wry smile had been replaced by a look of mild concern. He called me over and ushered me into his parlour with the offer of a glass of Mirinda fizzy orange. It was the best offer I'd had since my arrival. After days of being stonewalled, finally there was a breach in the Paradesi defences. Ironically, the breach had been made by the warden himself.

'Sit. Drink,' instructed Gamy, as his diminutive servant Mary laid out refreshments on paper napkins. 'What you need to know? I've got five minutes.'

*

What was the history that Sammy was so desperate to bury? The White Jews, save for Gamy, who was really a Black Jew who married one of the 'others', fell silent when asked about the past. Yet the problem between the Black and the White Jews was central to understanding why the Cochin Jews had come to a premature end.

Gamy and Reema were the exception not the rule, and their mixed marriage was accepted only now, when the end was in sight. For centuries marriage between the Blacks and the Whites had been taboo. The two communities were distinct and the Blacks were effectively barred from the Whites' synagogue. That more than anything rankled still. At the heart of the division was the argument over who came first, who were the real Jews of Cochin. While Sammy offered

a sanitized account of the past, for the Black Jews of Ernakulam, the shadows of past grievances merely lengthened with the passage of time.

Sammy may not have wanted to disclose his version of that history, but it was laid out for all to see in a series of simple mural paintings in the antechamber of the Paradesi Synagogue. The pictures with brief captions beneath told the Paradesis' official story: they were the ones who hailed back to the days of Solomon, they were the first to land in Kerala, their ancestor was the reputed elder and founding father Joseph Rabban. There was no mention of another community of Black Jews across the water in Ernakulam. Each year streams of visitors from around the world came to see the Paradesi Synagogue and its murals. As far as those visitors were concerned, this was the whole truth.

Central to the identity and mythology of the Kerala Jews – whether Black or White – is a place called Cranganore, also known as Shingly. Just as Jerusalem lies at the core of Jewish identity, so Cranganore is the centre of Cochini Jewish identity. The ruler was the so-called King of Shingly, Joseph Rabban, an elder welcomed like a raja by the people of Kerala when he first arrived. He has an almost mythological place in the heart of the community and its history, not unlike that of King David in Jerusalem.

The two cities are twinned in the historical narrative of Cochini Jews. Jerusalem was sacked, leading to the dispersal of the Jews in 70 CE. And a natural disaster and war drove out the Kerala Jews from their first kingdom, leading them to

resettle in Cochin. The pain of exile from Jerusalem is matched by the banishment from Cranganore. To this day the Cochini Jews will not visit Cranganore unless absolutely necessary. If they have no choice, they are careful to leave before sunset, fearing disaster will befall them if they remain once darkness sets in. Cranganore remains a city synonymous with tragedy, where the twin spectres of death and banishment still linger. Yet in recognition of its symbolic importance, every one of the community is still buried with a handful of earth from Cranganore, in memory of those first settlers.

Just as the Cochini Jews were keen to prove they hailed from Israel, so they were also keen to prove they came from the line of the first Jews to settle at Cranganore. Such lineage conferred status, a purity of heritage. Purity of heritage was also hugely important in Hinduism and those who were seen as the oldest and purest among the Jews were accorded greatest respect by the Brahmin classes of Kerala. Moreover, in Hindu India, status translated into economic and political power. For these reasons, the need to prove a link with Jerusalem and Cranganore was vital.

In *A Jewish King at Shingly*, authors Nathan Katz and Ellen Goldberg write about the 'symbolic intertwining of Jerusalem and Cranganore'. They also note that 'there was a sibling-like rivalry between the Paradesi and Malabari Jews over who were the rightful heirs of the line of Rabban' and his ancient kingdom.

But who was Joseph Rabban? Centuries after he landed in Malabar, his legacy is the subject of this tug of war. Inside the

Paradesi Synagogue antechamber, Rabban features centre stage in the paintings that depict the 'history' of the Jews of Cochin.

The early paintings show Shingly as their own city. One mural depicts a teeming bazaar, with the caption reading: 'There was trade between King Solomon's Palestine and the Malabar Coast.' That much is fact. The next painting shows the destruction of the Second Temple after which the Jews of the holy city scattered to all the compass points. The third painting shows a ship settling on a lush coastline. 'Landing of the Jews at Shingly,' reads the legend beneath.

The series then leaps several centuries forward to a seminal moment – the arrival of the legendary patriarch. An Indian king greets a shipload of Jewish migrants on their arrival in Kerala, bedecked in as lavish finery as any maharajah could muster, with full entourage bearing coloured parasols and beating drums. 'The Raja of Cranganore receives the Jews,' declares the solemn caption. The leader of the Jews is then portrayed in the audience chamber of the raja's palace, receiving a gift from the kingdom. This marks the real arrival of the Jews in Cochini society, no longer just another class of immigrant trading serfs, but now a favoured people in their adoptive land.

Little of the Cochini Jews' history is documented, but the story of their special status under the raja is recorded by one key artefact: a set of copper plates engraved with a royal decree. Cochini tradition says the plates were given to Joseph Rabban in 379 CE and they represent the clearest evidence of the antiquity of this community. The Paradesi elders say the

original plates are kept in the Ark inside their synagogue, but scholars differ in opinion on their age, with some dating them as late as 1000 CE.

The plates state that the Hindu king of Malabar awarded Rabban the village of Anjuvannam and its revenues as well as according him the right to certain privileges of the ruling class, such as riding an elephant, being carried aloft on a palanquin and being shielded by his very own state parasol. The three small rectangular copper plates are engraved in an ancient Tamil language written in the Vetteluttu script. A translation reads:

> Hail and Prosperity. The following gift was graciously made by him who had assumed the title King of Kings. His majesty the King Shri Parkaran Iravi Vanmar whose ancestors have been wielding the sceptre for many hundred thousand years... was pleased to make the following gifts: We have granted Joseph Rabban the village of Anjuvannam together with propriety rights, tolls on boats and carts, the revenue and the title of Anjuvannam, the lamp of the day, cloth spread in front to walk on a palanquin, a parasol, a Vaduga drum, trumpet, a gateway, a garland, decoration with festoons and so forth. We have granted him the land tax and the weight tax; moreover we have sanctioned with these copper plates that he need not pay the dues which the inhabitants of the other cities pay the Royal Palace and that he may enjoy the benefits they enjoy.

The gift of Anjuvannam was made in perpetuity to Rabin's successors, or as the charter poetically phrases it: 'so long as the world and moon exist'.

The Jews' charter was unique in that it granted them rights that were usually the preserve of the royal family alone, including firing three salutes at daybreak and on the day of a marriage. Naturally, both sides of the Cochini Jewish family wanted to claim Rabban as their own, eulogizing him in word and song. He who hailed from Joseph Rabban hailed from a line of kings.

In the Malayalam folk songs, recorded by the women of the community in handwritten notebooks and handed down the generations, there is a wedding song that likens Joseph Rabban to a handsome bridegroom. These songs are a musical history of the people, so it is unsurprising that Joseph Rabban, their idealized first man, should feature so prominently. The lyrics of one wedding song say that on the day of marriage 'the bridegroom is like Joseph Rabban, he is like a king'.

To the Jews of Kerala, Joseph Rabban was everything: founding father; groom to the bride, Cochin's Jewish people; and King of the Jews in this realm of the East.

A link back to this Jewish King of Shingly was proof of purity. The White Jews insisted that they were the true descendants of this line and I guessed that in a way Sammy saw himself as the natural inheritor of Joseph Rabban. Any questioning of this truth, the truth of the Paradesi Jews, was a questioning of the position of both Sammy Hallegua and his ancestors.

But there was a second, even more controversial test of Jewish status for the Paradesi community: colour. The white-skinned Jews claimed their very pallor was proof of purity.

Their people had predominately hailed from Europe: many of their number arrived in India after fleeing religious persecution during the Inquisition of the sixteenth century. On reaching the Malabar coastline they found another older community of Jews, but one which was darker skinned and fully integrated with the local Cochini people. Some of those European Jews married Jews who originated from Cranganore. But there was evidence of tensions mounting between the Black and White communities early on. David Mandelbaum, an academic who studied the Cochini Jewry extensively in the twentieth century, wrote of how the European Jews on their arrival in India found it difficult to relate to their brethren, who differed in so many ways.

Keen to distinguish themselves, the Paradesis claimed they had never been polluted by non-Jewish blood. They claimed to have a deeper understanding of the Torah and Jewish knowledge and sought to distance themselves in order to win a higher place in the caste-based society of Cochin. Just as the higher caste members of Hindu society in Kerala segregated themselves from others on the basis of religious purity and superiority, so the Paradesis distanced themselves from the Malabari Jews.

Their facility with European languages and trade links with the West positioned them well with the royal court, allowing them to propagate their version of history not just to

the local dignitaries but also to influential visitors. In the four hundred years that followed their arrival in the sixteenth century, they would spread the story that the Black Jews, already well established in the region, were not 'pure' but the sons of slaves who had come on the ships of Solomon and then married local Cochini women, thereby polluting the Jewish maternal bloodline.

The taint of slavery in caste-based Kerala proved devastating and would lead to the decline of the Malabaris in Cochini society. Claims that the Malabaris were somehow lesser Jews naturally outraged the people of Ernakulam and its surrounding villages, whose ancestors had attended the old 'southside' synagogue that once existed in Cranganore. They found their beloved ancestral figure Joseph Rabban had been hijacked by the newcomers. To this day the Black Jews claim the copper plates housed in the Paradesi Synagogue were stolen from them way back in their history, although they have no proof of this. More fundamentally, the Blacks found themselves usurped in their own historical narrative – a story that went back to Joseph Rabban and his fateful meeting with the raja in Cranganore, then back further still to the days of King Solomon. The Malabaris believed it was they who hailed from kings. The holy cities of Jerusalem and Cranganore were their inheritance and the betrayal by the Paradesi Jews had now placed all this under threat.

So the battle lines were drawn, coursing through the brackish green waters that separated Mattancheri and Ernakulam. As the Whites fought ruthlessly for pre-eminence

in Cochini society, the scene was set for the introduction of a policy of colour separation, a Jewish apartheid in India that would last for four centuries and eventually lead to the decline and fall of both Black and White.

Three

The End of Shalom

'May all blessings be upon you;
May you be blessed with children and shalom.
Be blessed and multiply in the earth.
Take possession to divide it, so that you may survive.'

A Cochini blessing from Jewish Women's Songs from
Kerala, as sung by Sarah Cohen and Ruby Hallegua

Shalom Cohen's funeral had sent ripples of foreboding
through this tiny community, awakening the old dread, un-
settling the mundane routines of life, its effect magnified
because the White Jews were so few in number. Each family
carried the burden in its own way, fiercely protective, guarded
against outsiders who would prey upon their tragedy. Among
the twelve who remained, there were no young lovers or
newly-weds, no sulky teenagers consumed with their own
selfish traumas, no rascal kids and chubby babies to lift the
elders from the mire of the past.

This was the strangest thing about life on Synagogue

Lane: everyone seemed to be in countdown mode: the Jews themselves were counting the number of those remaining, taking mental bets on who might be next. The Muslims and Christians on this street were counting their profits or the potential profits to be made from this dying and world-famous community. Soon, Synagogue Lane would no longer be home to the White Jews, but an anthropological curiosity, with boarded houses up for grabs to be turned into souvenir shops or cafés for the tourists. The prey and the predator shared Synagogue Lane, their fortunes entwined.

It was difficult to speak of the Kerala Jews without the epithet 'last'. The last young Jew, the last young Jewess, the last *shohet*, the last working synagogue, the last marriage and the last birth on the street, which was so long ago no one could rightly remember.

Sarah was the 'last' of the Cohens, the family that drew its name from the priestly line of the *kohanim*. Moreover she was the last of her household: first her parents, then her husband and now her brother had passed away. Hers had been a barren marriage, so the house was empty of heirs and now her servants and hangers-on were plotting to wrest this pricey piece of real estate from her grasp.

Strangely enough, when I first arrived, no one wanted to talk to me except for Sarah. My thoughts seemed to resonate with hers. Having Shalom taken from her so unexpectedly had brought to the surface reflections about what was left, for her, her people and how it had come to this point.

Sarah's house sits at the very top of Synagogue Lane, near

the first Kashmiri tourist shops. The windows of her house were protected with grilles depicting the Star of David and painted in red, white and a sky blue. During the day the hall-way of her house was converted into a shop selling embroidered goods.

She sat in a chair by the door in a small rectangle of yellow sunlight, her knees slightly apart, toes idly twiddling on the cool tiled floor. A copy of the Torah was open in her lap, its pages flapping in the breeze as she stared into the distance. This was her favourite spot: sitting inside the doorway, looking out on to the street. From here Sarah knew she would miss nothing and hear everything. From here she would note the caravan of tourists and passers-by on their way to the synagogue, straining to catch stray gossip like a child netting butterflies.

The shutter doors of her house were open, leading to a long narrow corridor, a darkened haven from the white heat. Inside were tables and rails laden with folded piles of embroidered Jewish *kippahs*, white silk tableware for special festivals, embroidered with golden and silver thread. At the back of her store was the more workaday stock: damask and linen tablecloths and napkin sets, embroidered with pink rosebuds and bordered in lace; gingham cotton dresses for small children, with frills and flounces in keeping with flamboyant southern Indian tastes. These and other goods were sold to tourists to bring in a little income now that she had no means of support.

I had seen and heard about Sarah from books, pictures

and stories about the community. Being the oldest surviving lady, she was the grand dame of Cochini White Jewry. Her husband had been Jacob or 'Dickie' Cohen, from one of the less well-off Paradesi families and a lawyer by training. A community leader, Dickie had been one of the few qualified under Jewish law to teach the younger boys about the faith. He died long ago, taking that tradition with him to the grave. The couple had been at the core of this community, a kind of Posh and Becks of Cochin: the 'it' couple who led the prayers and the partying that used to be part and parcel of Cochini Jewish life.

Today I found an old woman who was a faded facsimile of that past, a worn-out spirit engulfed by grief. Shalom was given the full traditional burial rites accorded to a member of the White Jewish community. Sarah described the traditions, sometimes slipping into generic descriptions of a Cochini funeral to lessen the pain of returning to that day in September 2006. His body was buried in the Jews' special graveyard just a few hundred metres away – a graveyard that had once forbidden the burial of their Black Jewish brethren alongside the Whites.

Despite being in mourning, Sarah seemed to welcome company, crave it even, and invited me to pull up a chair and share her ringside view. As a young woman, she had been a vivacious creature, with a lusty gap-toothed smile that had captivated Dickie all those years ago. I got the sense that theirs had been a passionate relationship. She was a young woman barely into her twenties, he a middle-aged man who fell for

the kid next door with the sexy figure and head of wild black curls. Sarah had never been a beauty, but she had an earthy quality that enabled her to ensnare one of Jew Town's most eligible men.

The fierce midday sunlight was a harsh judge as it fell upon her face, making her squint irritably. Her long countenance was lengthened further by crepe-like folds of skin that hung from her jaw-line, her mouth and eyes etched with deep lines that told stories of tremendous happiness as well as pain. Her skin remained a creamy luminescent white despite the intense Kerala heat. She retained her wiry curls, now steel grey instead of black. Grief and time had played mischief with her health and looks, drawing dark circles around drooping eyes.

She was dressed in white, wearing a sleeveless top which exposed fleshy arms, and a striped cotton sarong tied about her waist. She cradled her right hand in her lap, keen to draw attention to it. A week ago, in careless distraction she had splashed boiling tea on herself, taking off the skin on the back of the hand, leaving it red-raw, with ragged brown edges fraying around the wound. 'I must not touch it,' she told me, touching it, 'or it will bleed.' She bit her bottom lip and then, with a sucking motion, she moved her dentures in and out, looking at me with mournful eyes.

She asked what I was doing in Cochin and explained that the Jews were in the midst of their autumn festivals. I had been warned before I came that the community was notoriously closed to the point of outright hostility, but luckily for

me, Sarah wanted to talk. Her conversation was candid, irreverent and invariably indiscreet. She said it was time the story was told. There was no point delaying, as these were the last days and one had to get the story on paper while there were still those left alive to tell it. Already she feared they had become no more than living museum pieces. Every day streams of tourists, Jew and non-Jew, Indian and foreign, paraded this street in gawping huddles, clad in the ubiquitous uniform of vest, hiking shorts and rucksack. One could see the Jews twitching with irritation from behind their lace curtains as they surveyed this defilement of their community. The tourists knew no bounds, poking their heads inside the doorways of the Jews' houses, scrutinizing the latest exhibit before moving on. Some came in genuine tribute, armed with information about the Jews' migration to these shores, and fascinated by their lasting endurance in India. Others were simply on the *Lonely Planet* tourist trail. After Synagogue Lane, came the local shops, an Ayurvedic massage and then lunch at the nearby coffee shop where Brad Pitt once hung out to drink lassi.

In the old days, the whole town had belonged to the Jews. No strangers came walking down their street, into their synagogue, let alone their homes. If they did, the occurrence was rare and sanctioned. Today tourism had almost become a *raison d'être*, with the synagogue already accorded future museum status by the Archaeological Survey of India.

'This was once our place, full of only our people,' said Sarah. 'Now after the others left, gone to Israel, gone overseas,

or just gone – the Kashmiris, the Muslims, the Christians have come. They're good people, they take care of us. But they're not our kind. The old life is gone.'

'What was it like, when you, Dickie and Shalom lived here, when it was all Jewish?'

'On festival nights we'd sing, visit each other's houses. The men would drink, tell jokes and old stories. The women would sing Cochini wedding songs, cook together for the festivals, play cards on tables set out in the street. Now, hardly ever do we sit out. And there's nobody to talk to. If there's a party, who'll come? The old, the dead?'

Shalom had been the older brother, but more than that, he had been a companion and friend. He was the first-born to the Cohen family in Jew Town, a well-to-do and educated family in the Paradesi community. There were four children: first Shalom, then Sarah, then another sister and a brother whose birth coincided with tragedy. All four were born in the house of Queenie, who came from a high Jewish family that held vast estates and property portfolios and had business interests across the region. When Queenie married Sammy, the two Paradesi dynasties and their riches were united.

After Sarah's youngest sibling was born, on the day of the baby's circumcision the mother was taken ill. 'In the evening my mother came home from the synagogue and began violently purging. The doctor was called and he gave her medicine but it didn't stop. After endless days of purging she died, leaving four small children.'

Stricken with grief, the father took Shalom to Bombay to

live and left the younger children, including Sarah, to be brought up by their grandparents on Synagogue Lane. So she lost both parents in quick succession. Her father remarried and Shalom grew up in Bombay and worked for the family's printing press. Business was good and the family's fortunes prospered, but her elder brother and father had become strangers.

With her male guardians far from home as she grew up, Sarah turned into a wilful young woman. In her twenties she caused a minor scandal when she defied her father by marrying her next-door neighbour, Dickie Cohen. It was his second marriage and some of the neighbours suggested in hushed tones that his love for Sarah pre-dated the death of Dickie's first and much older wife. But Sarah remained unapologetic.

'I was in love. We lived in the same town, on the same street; we saw each other every day. We fell in love. It was like that. Father didn't like it, so he came and took me to Bombay.'

Dickie was not the kind of man who gave up. He pursued Sarah to Bombay, where she lived the dull life of the dutiful daughter, within the confines prescribed by her father. Dickie rescued her and the couple escaped into the pulsating metropolis, where they married in reckless defiance of her father's wishes. They returned to Jew Town as man and wife and set up home, their love an open challenge to the elders. Here was a man who on paper seemed the perfect suitor. Why had her father been so opposed?

'This was Dickie's second marriage. In a way, that was

nothing important: he was a Jew, he was a lawyer, and he was a Cohen. There was nothing wrong with him, no reason why I shouldn't marry him. He was also very good-looking. He followed me to Bombay, we got married. Finished.'

Their love was exclusive and remained so, until Shalom joined their household years later after the death of his father. He never married and so moved in with Sarah and her husband. By then the rest of the family had left, so the three lived happily under the same roof for their remaining years. When Dickie passed away, the bond between brother and sister grew stronger. Shalom and Sarah were one another's closest friend and confidant. So when Shalom suffered a fall a few months ago and entered the coma from which he never recovered, the impact on Sarah was devastating; as if the ground beneath had suddenly given way, plunging her into grief's abyss.

We could hear the bolt straining against her main door. It had started to pour, the rain coming down in gusting sheets that caused rivulets of dark water to swell and overflow from the guttering, rushing down the street. The pungent smell of damp earth rose from outside and entered through the open windows, engulfing us with its sweet muskiness. The guests at the door were the nightwatchman and one of the old servants from the town – both Christians. They had come for their regular evening's viewing of the Malayalam soap opera that began at 7.30 p.m. With Sarah they would normally settle down in the living room in front of the TV each night, she sharing her relative wealth with them, regardless of religion

and caste. In the past the White Jews attached great importance to such things as status and their in-bred superiority, but an increased vulnerability had made them more accommodating.

The two settled down in the other room – the old woman in a white sari neatly folded her skinny limbs on the windowsill like a rag doll, the watchman perched on a chair in the corner directly opposite the TV, a bag of gram nuts in his lap and legs akimbo – and became absorbed in the dramatized epic about the Hindu god Lord Krishna. Sarah and I returned to the back room, with the sound of the ululating Malayalam drama pulsating through the house like a crazy heartbeat while the rain drummed relentlessly outside. Sarah resumed her place at the table and piled more food on to my plate. The simple act of serving me triggered memories of mealtimes with her brother. In memory of lost loved ones, it is said that the Jews will sometimes set places for the dead at table.

'I really miss him most now,' she told me, 'at the time of my food.' Her voice became small, like a child's, as she wiped away tears and then blew her nose into the tea towel. 'When we used to sit here, when I'd eat especially, I always liked to push the dishes to him. "Shalom. Eat," I'd tell him.' She pushed imaginary plates in my direction. 'I liked to watch him taste the dishes. I liked to watch him eat until he became full. I'd tell him when the synagogue services were happening, when there were festival prayers, who was visiting, who was leaving. In the evening, I'd tell him when Johnny and Sammy had gone to the synagogue and say, "Shalom, dress up, come."'

'Did he like the synagogue?'

'He'd always wear his best suit to go there. Always, the best suit.' She paused to blow her nose again.

'He sounded like a fine man,' I said, feeling with each passing moment like a vulture feasting on the sorrows of strangers.

'He was a fine man,' she continued, her spaniel eyes alighting for the first time since we'd met. 'A quiet fellow. Never used to fight with anybody. When anybody came he would talk. He got on with anyone. That was Shalom's way.'

Without prompting she recounted the night of the accident; words, details, feelings, pieces of a nightmare that cascaded from her memory, until that evening was laid bare before us: 'It was just another night, we had dinner, we talked, we went upstairs. As usual, I went off to bed. After an hour or so I saw Shalom hadn't come back from the toilet, so I thought maybe he's purging or he wet his pants. I got up. Shalom is not here, Shalom has not come, I tell myself.' Her eyes were now looking beyond me, beyond this room.

The design of the Jewish houses on Synagogue Lane is unusual. They have a linking corridor or room on the upper floor that allows families from one house to come into the neighbouring home if needed. That night in a panic, Sarah called out to Gamy's wife Reema, who lived next door.

'Luckily, Reema was awake at 10.30 p.m. I called out. She said to go down and open the door and see where he'd gone. I went down the stairs, just two steps, and there, at the foot of the stairs, I saw Shalom on the floor in a pool of blood.

His head was cut from here to here,' she indicated with her right hand a huge gash across his skull. 'He had no sickness, nothing to complain of. No asthma, no pressure. Nothing. He was that healthy. Then this! Straight away I took him to the hospital.'

Shalom was in a deep coma. Two months after the fall his condition deteriorated and he died. It was a stupid accident and a pointless death. The funeral rites lasted several days and he was buried in the cemetery reserved for the White Jews. Sammy, the synagogue warden, and his brother Johnny led the duties on the men's side. As was her duty, Sarah bought the white material that was stitched into a shroud. 'I took my machine into the synagogue to stitch it. The men of the synagogue had the duty of giving the last bath to Shalom's body, a purification rite. In this way, we pulled together.'

Shalom's abrupt departure underlined the frailty of those left. His death was the last in a series of losses for Sarah which began decades ago with the breaking up of her community following the creation of Israel.

'It began thirty, forty years ago. When the Cochini Jews decided to pack up and go, they sold their houses – to pay for the travel to Israel. One by one we watched the houses being sold. As a girl, the noise on this street was incredible. We were such a loud community, too much noise, I'd say. We were never scared. Now we're scared.'

It seemed a strange choice of word. 'Why scared?' I asked.

'Because we feel lonely. A terrible loneliness, to lose your people, to know the end is coming. Our neighbours, the

Muslims, the Kashmiris, are good friends to us, but there's nobody here when they close their shops at night. They close and go home. Nobody among them lives here, not a single person.

'These last few years have seen too much stress. It's we who must bury our last friends, close our synagogue for ever one day soon, watch our houses sold to speculators. This is why sometimes Sammy and the others get angry. Angry at outsiders who come to watch us die. Angry at those who abandoned us.'

'You blame those who left?' I asked, skipping over the fact that I was here for exactly that – to witness their demise.

'What can we feel?' she murmured softly. 'They're determined to go, they'll go. Let them go. We remain here. Finished.'

'If life was so good for the Jews, why did so many leave? You seemed to have it all.'

'It's true, we were happy, very happy,' she agreed, sucking her dentures in contemplation. She pushed the lower palate out of its socket so that it protruded from her lips before snapping it back into place. 'But, see, those who passed out from college, they found no jobs here. Abroad they'll get a job. Some went to Israel, some went from Israel to America. And the young ones, where were the partners? Husbands, wives? For these reasons, they had to go.'

There were still a few youngsters left, both Black and White, so why didn't they come together and marry to allow the old Cochini line to continue? It was a loaded question, as

I knew the old resentment still festered. The Paradesi Jews were afraid of how history would judge their treatment of their fellow Jews across the water: cast out from their synagogue because of colour, an act that went against the essence of Judaism, the sense of justice that was the source of shalom. Sarah summed up the past succinctly:

'The Whites stuck to our own. The Blacks, the same. Besides, what young people do we have here? We've just one or two and they can't stand one another. If we force the topic of marriage, they go wild. We cannot force them. We've given up.'

'So, this is it,' I said, all of a sudden poisoned by the pessimism around me, the oppressive drumming of the rain overhead, and the idea of spending my evening with one Jewish and two Christian pensioners watching a Hindu religious epic in Malayalam. 'After all that's happened, millennia of history, from Solomon's Israel to twenty-first-century India, it will end. Just like that.'

'What are you talking?' she said irritably, as she reached for another pakora, crumbs scattering from her lips like bitter words. 'It's ended already. Even now we don't have enough men to hold Shabbat. Without the people from Ernakulum, there'd be no prayers on festival. We can't eat meat unless their *shohet* cuts it first. *They* only are keeping us alive.'

The White Jews of Synagogue Lane were on a life-support mechanism, kept alive by their old rivals. The Paradesis had gone from living on the same street, eating from the same plate, sharing the same synagogue, in and out of one another's

houses, being part of every development of one another's lives, from birth to bar mitzvah, from marriage to funeral, to this – something beyond death. The end of their history. The end of shalom.

Four

The Gentle Executioner

'A man's table is like the altar.'

The Talmud, Hagigah 27a

History has a habit of biting back. There was a time when the Paradesi Jews refused to eat kosher meat that was killed by a Black Jewish hand. The Paradesis had their own butcher, or *shohet*, and the Malabaris theirs. When Dickie Cohen died, Synagogue Lane lost its *shohet* and the only kosher slaughterer who remained was Elias 'Babu' Joseph, a Black Jew from Ernakulam. If the Paradesis wanted to eat meat, then they had to take meat cut by Babu's hand. The irony was not lost on Babu, a man who felt keenly the injuries of the past.

Babu is the last *shohet* for the Cochini Jewry and after him there is nobody to take his place. I arranged to meet him at his place of business, Cochin Blossoms, just off Jew Street in Ernakulam, an aquarium and garden centre housed in a disused synagogue. Jew Street was once the exclusive enclave of the local Jewish community and all the houses and local

businesses were owned by their people. Today it is a religious mix, with just a handful of families remaining amidst Muslims, Hindus and Christians. There are two synagogues here, one of which is still in use for special occasions once or twice a year, when visiting Jews help to make up the quorum for prayers. In contrast, a few doors down, off a narrow alleyway, the local mosque is packed at prayer daily. Five times a day the cry of namaaz echoes through the old Jewish quarter.

Babu's shop was around the corner from Jew Street, in the antechamber of Ernakulam's disused second synagogue. The synagogue was engulfed by the hullabaloo of the local bazaar, a mostly pedestrian zone where one can buy all manner of goods, from electrical items to copper-bottomed cooking pots, bolts of block-printed cotton to fluttering silk kaftans. 'Kerala Fancy Goods', 'The Lungi Emporium' and 'The Exclusive International Handbag Company' are just some of the hand-painted signs overhanging the dense thoroughfare thronged with honking tongas, rickshaws and pitiful mules, bent low beneath their parcels like put-upon husbands.

Amidst the chaotic sprawl of stores, stalls and twisting alleys bristling with shoppers was the old Tekkumbagam synagogue. The narrow path was lined with potted plants, casting a dappled shadow overhead. The courtyard outside the large stone and timber building was filled with row upon row of flowers, palms, creeping vines with white blossoms, seedlings of geranium, bougainvillea and herbs. Each plant was lovingly nourished with water and shielded from the harsh sunlight with a green netting canopy.

Up the stone steps and through huge wooden doors was a shady haven filled with banks of fish tanks that had an immediate calming effect. Babu's desk and chair were positioned exactly opposite the entrance, giving him a clear view of all visitors. The desk was spread with papers, brochures on the latest exotic fish and fish husbandry, lists of local suppliers and so on. On the desk shelf he had a row of glass pots filled with tight bundles of Chinese bamboo, bound in red tinsel, for good luck and prosperity.

His aquarium empire lay behind: scores of tanks filled with bubbling green water and fish. Some were water-borne jewels of bright red and yellow, the size of a finger nail. Others were aquatic birds of paradise, with plume-like fins fanning out in shimmering display. The tanks were clean and well aerated and the fish looked well cared for, loved even. Clearly this was more than a matter of profit and loss. Babu gave his fish life and in turn they bestowed a kind of peace. His prize specimen was the endangered Arowana, the legendary dragon fish of Asia. The fish is highly prized and auspicious, considered to be lucky in some countries. It is a collector's piece. The full-grown Arowana looked like a Supreme Court judge, with its distinguished whiskers and jutting jaw, parading majestically up and down its own super-size tank. In a nearby smaller tank was a younger, green Arowana, a quarter of the size. Despite its best efforts, it lacked the majesty of the full-grown version, rather like a young man hopelessly trying to emulate his father by sporting a downy moustache.

From the ceiling, along with coloured glass lanterns, hung

packets of plastic toys and plants to landscape the fish tanks. Babu's employees, a bunch of wiry-limbed Muslim boys, were unpacking boxes when I arrived. They removed clear plastic bags filled with water and new stocks of fish and the shop floor was transformed into a surreal scene: aisles filled with scores of gently bobbling balloons of water, each cradling its own multi-coloured shoal of exotic fish. The balloons gently lolled from side to side, bumping one another, like giant soap bubbles. One by one, the boys took the bags, popped them open and decanted the fish into tanks.

Babu was a tall, strong-looking man, with kind brown eyes, dark polished skin and thick, neatly cut salt-and-pepper hair. He was forty-nine years old and married to a Bene Israel Jewess called Ofra. They had two daughters aged eighteen and fifteen and the family was part of the twenty-two Jews that lived in Ernakulam.

The disused Tekkumbagam synagogue at the back of his aquarium was built in remembrance of the first synagogue in Cranganore, known as the 'southside' synagogue because of its location on the river. It could be reached through doors at the back of the aquarium. The doorway was partially blocked by sacks of fish feed and other supplies, but once inside the synagogue chamber, I was struck by its particular beauty – simpler, more austere and yet just as arresting as the synagogue in Mattancheri. The Tekkumbagam Synagogue has ten windows representing the commandments and two pillars evoking the pillars at the entrance of the Temple of Solomon.

The place was in shadow as the shutters remained bolted.

Instead of the smell of oil lamps and incense there was the aroma of neglect, where there were once garlands of jasmine, cobwebs now dangled in silver tapestries from beams overhead. When this synagogue was still active, the Jewish children were taught Bible classes in the antechamber. This particular community did not have rabbis, but scholars known as *hamim*. The Jewish children learned the Torah, as well as the old Shingly songs, poems and Hebrew. They came not just on Sabbath, but every day after school. The synagogue was the epicentre, the source of knowledge, meaning and life. As the Jewish community diminished over the years and the need for a place of worship became redundant, Babu took over and converted part of the building. In deference to its past, he did not touch the place of worship itself, merely converting the front part into his aquarium. Its Ark remained, but the copies of the Torah were removed and sent to Israel long ago. So, where Jewish children once sat cross-legged on the flagstone floor to recite the Torah, their curled ringlets bobbing at their ears as they prayed, tanks of tropical fish now resided in desiccated splendour.

Babu slipped a brown paper bag into his trouser pocket and a blue *kippah* cap in the other. 'Now we must go,' he said, striding towards the door. On the Thursday morning before the weekend of Simhat Torah, I joined the last remaining *shohet* in action at Cochini market for the slaughter of the chickens.

Every few weeks or in the run-up to a major festival, the White Jews send an Ambassador taxi to Babu's aquarium

which is a forty-minute drive from Mattancheri. The taxi driver hands over a fold of rupee notes to pay for the chickens that Babu must purchase and then slaughter for the White community. In the run-up to Simhat Torah, one of the biggest celebrations of the year, each community was busy preparing for a lavish banquet. Babu was tasked with cutting the meat for the White Jews and sending it back in plastic bags in the taxi.

It was just one example of how the Black and White Jews had become mutually dependent in their twilight years: forced to co-operate so a *minyan* of ten men may be formed in the Paradesi synagogue for special festivals, so they may eat meat at their now infrequent banquets, in rare communion for a few days of the year. The two communities reminded me of a quarrelling old couple, cherishing old grievances, harking back to past betrayals, yet sticking by one another in age and adversity because there was no one else.

The Cochin market itself was a gourmand's paradise, with great sacks packed tight with spices that tickled the senses: cardamom, jeera, turmeric, chilli powder, cloves, star anise, cinnamon sticks. Also on sale were roughly broken pieces of the natural brown sweetener jaggery, used in cakes and desserts. Sesame-seed-encrusted ladoos in trays and cling film, plastic bowls bobbing with saffron-drenched *rasmalai* and syrupy gulab jamun. Mounds of tender green coconuts, papaya, watermelon, bunches of tiny black seedless grapes and every type of banana imaginable – red, green, large extra gelatinous yellow, and the tiny yellow finger-sized bananas

that are most prized. Wicker baskets of green gooseberries the size of plums, bulbous and delicately veined like plucked eyeballs. All manner of vegetable fuelled the appetite: tiny sweet potatoes little bigger than the tip of one's thumb, bundles of spinach and the bitter green methi, fragrant bouquets of dhania and mint, gleaming aubergines and cartloads of red onions, tomatoes and garlic, the staples of the Indian kitchen.

Beyond this section was a large courtyard jostling with fishmongers, men and women, lungis and skirts hoisted above the knees as they squatted low over stone gullies which carried the blood and dirty water into the drains. The workers cleaned, gutted and stacked piles of glistening silver sardines, mullet and pomfret as well as rarer catch such as sea bass. Grey pyramids of fresh prawn and shrimp dried on newspapers alongside aluminium bowls of round clams the size of a penny coin and crabs that would fit in the small palm of a child. The cacophony of fishwives bartering in Malayalam was deafening.

Beyond the fish section was the meat quarter, where hunks of mutton marbled with bright yellow fat hung from hooks over butchers' counters, swinging pendulously in the shimmering heat. At the very back of this compound, up a flight of steps, was the live chicken quarter – the smell of feathers and the butcher's block hit you before the sight of scores of wire and wooden chicken coops, packed to bursting point with white chickens. The coops were stacked in a square around a central workstation, a roughly hewn table of hardwood

stained with dried blood. A pile of old giblets sat in one corner, waiting to be cleared away, providing a bloody feast for the fat black flies that swarmed busily.

There was an old-fashioned set of scales to weigh the birds. The birds selected for the Jewish table must be of the same weight and size, without any physical defect or blemish. Even after slaughter, if a bird is found to have some internal ailment, the entire carcass is jettisoned. Around thirty fowl had been selected and set aside in a separate pen. As I arrived, the dreadful lottery of death came to a close as the last few birds were selected and drawn in squawking dismay to be weighed.

Babu stepped up to the butcher's block and a hush prevailed. It was as if the chickens knew their executioner had arrived. He was silent, dignified, mentally preparing himself for the religious duty ahead. He took out his blue cotton *kippah* and placed it on his head before carefully removing the special blade from its brown paper and sharpening it slowly, one side, then the other, with great deliberation across a whetstone. He was assisted by one of the market men, a Hindu, who prepared a jug of water and stood opposite Babu. Two other boys, also non-Jewish, waited by the chopping counter, their hatchets ready to skin and carve up the birds once the kosher ceremony was completed.

Babu's assistant removed the first bird from the cage. Its terror was palpable, eyes bulging, wings flapping frantically. The screeching reverberated through the market as the other chickens watched in silence, heads cocked.

Babu began the Hebrew prayer that must precede the

killing, praying for the life that God gave, the life he was about to take away. The assistant dipped the chicken's head into the jug of water, forcing it to take water and swallow. The reflex action made the bird's jugular vein stand out in its neck and as the assistant held the body and wings, Babu pulled the head towards him, stretching its neck and securing the thick vein and cartilage between his finger and thumb. Silenced, the bird looked unblinkingly into Babu's eyes as gently yet firmly he sliced the bird's neck in three short cuts of the blade. It was over in less than a second and the chicken's limp body was laid on the chopping block, its soft white feathers drenched crimson with blood. One of the boys took the bird's carcass. It was de-feathered, skinned and butchered into pieces within the minute.

Babu and his assistants continued the production line of slaughter until within thirty minutes all the fowl were killed and cut. During the entire process Babu's face remained a mask of impassivity and he spoke not a word. After it was over, he took his blade, washed it down in a fresh jug of water and then poured the pink, blood-stained contents on to the stone floor. He wiped down the blade, removed the brown paper sheath from his pocket and slid the blade back in. Then he washed and dried his hands, removed the *kippah*, folded it and tucked it into his other trouser pocket. As he completed his ritual, Babu's gaze fell to the ground where tiny dark spots of blood stared up at him like accusatory eyes of the dead.

*

An hour later we were settled in chairs in the green coolness of the aquarium again. On our return, we had been waylaid in the fish section of the market as Babu's eye was caught by a spectacular sea bass weighing in at six kilos and glisteningly fresh. The festival season was upon us and this weekend marked two of the most important dates in the Jewish calendar, Shmini and Simhat Torah, so Babu wanted to buy something special for dinner. He agreed a price of 1,050 rupees. The specimen, he pronounced, was perfect in age, weight and texture, as we watched it being wrapped up like fish groupies. 'Such a fish doesn't come along every day,' Babu explained with quiet excitement.

As soon as we were settled in his office he made a flurry of calls to local families and agreed to split the cost with them and share the delicacy for the special festival dinner. Already there was a sense of excitement building, like the run-up to Diwali or Christmas. It was a far cry from the White Jews of Synagogue Lane, enveloped in a fog of despondency, where the synagogue warden stomped the streets in ill temper and impatience. Sammy would also be hosting a party on Friday night to celebrate the beginning of the festival of Shmini. In attendance would be the great and good of Cochin, non-Jews. The other Jews on his street were invited for a drink, but many said they would not attend the dinner.

In the past, Sammy's late father-in-law, Sattu Koder, hosted parties for all the Jewish neighbours as well. The street was alive with celebrations or parties for days. When the old warden died, the effervescence of those nights was also

extinguished and today each family preferred to return home for a special meal and toast in their own house.

But the Ernakulam Jews still prayed together and partied together on all special occasions. This Friday night, after prayers, they planned to sit down at one table for dinner. It had been so in the past and it remained so still; hence the air of expectation and Babu's delight in securing his sea bass. As we discussed the preparations, Babu visibly relaxed, eased into his chair and exuded serenity, in keeping with his garden and aquarium.

The conversation turned to whether the Black and White Jews would be celebrating together over the coming days and Babu explained that such unions were rare. The old insults still burned. As he sipped his chai, looking out over the garden, the softness in his eyes was replaced by a fire I had not seen until now: 'What bullshit they talk,' he murmured softly.

'We're the first Jews in Kerala. Our ancestors came from Cranganore, our history dates back to the beginning. I can show you a tombstone of one of our people that dates back to the thirteenth century. They freely admit their ancestors came from Europe only in the fifteenth century. So how can they be first?'

The tombstone he referred to was the oldest Jewish gravestone in Kerala. It was dated 1269 and was in the tiny Malabari village of Chennamangalam. There the Jews had once lived under the protection of a local chieftain called the Paliat Achan. The tombstone, written in Hebrew, stands

outside the Chennamangalam Synagogue, which has been renovated and is now a museum.

'If it's so evident,' I asked, 'why do many still believe they are the original Jews of Cochin?'

'Because people go to them, to the other Jew Town, they listen to one side of the story, a partial history, and they believe the Whites were the first and only Jews. They swallow this story. But it's bullshit. I'm sorry for this language, but I've no other word,' he said. 'They choose not to recognize an older community just forty minutes away in Ernakulam. One that was larger than theirs and longer in tradition in Kerala. Instead, we're subjected to this humbug that they're the first and true Jews.'

It was awkward, but I asked about the Paradesi claim that the Malabari Jews were descended from slaves. The question was like lighting the touch-paper on a Diwali firecracker.

'They call us sons of slaves. It makes me angry when they say this. Our ancestor was the great Joseph Rabban and, before that, the Jewish merchants who came to India after the fall of the Second Temple in Jerusalem. Our line goes back to the Holy City itself. They can only truly say for sure their line goes back to Spain. Yet, because they're rich, because they have the white skin, their story is more exotic, more romantic. It's swallowed whole, no questions.'

Babu's blood pressure was up and he needed to take tea to calm down. An aquarium was a good place for him to be, a kind of occupational therapy. So much for the Paradesis' claim that the old Black–White tensions were over. Babu

passed his hand over his moustaches, swiftly brushing them back and forth as he gathered his thoughts before lifting the glass to his lips. The chai did its work, slaking his thirst and soothing his anger.

'I was taught Hebrew by my father, you know. My mother, who's very orthodox, insisted. She was a tough lady. He taught me little, I admit, so I can't teach my own children. But it's the same with the White Jews, now they've no hereditary priest. They've no scholars. The last true scholar was Jacob Cohen. Now, he was a man of their community I admired. Jacob Cohen was a man with a sharp mind, a wonderful person, a genius, a great teacher. It was he who told me to learn to cut the chicken in the kosher way. He was the only man who could do so and he said to me, "One day I will die and go and who will cut the chicken for the Jews then? You must learn, you must carry on. I'll teach you."

'For three years he taught me. I was in my mid-thirties. Jacob could see far into the future, he could predict the problems. He blamed Koder, Queenie's father, and said because of him the community was dying. Koder was a rich man and he could have helped more people, then maybe more would have stayed. His daughter Queenie married her first cousin Sammy, from another wealthy family but with nothing like Koder's wealth. This is their way – to keep the skin pure but, more important, to keep the money inside the family. This history of intermarriage, interbreeding, what has it led to? This refusal to marry Black Jews? It has led to death. To

their diminishment, to a tiny group of people who are brilliant but without purpose, too eccentric or in some cases just mad. Many are unmarried, many are without children. How can such a community go on?'

Babu explained how most of the people on both sides of the water were poor. Not everyone had the riches of the Koders and Halleguas, or even the modest wealth of Babu. For these people, Israel had represented not just a spiritual return, but a chance to start over.

'For them the State of Israel was a Promised Land in more than one way. It really was a land of milk and honey. So they went for a better life. What to lose?'

Just as the youngsters had fled Mattancheri, Babu feared the last young Jews of Ernakulam would also be pulled away by the forces of economics – that and the quest for love.

'Of our twenty-two people, the youngest is my daughter who's fifteen,' he said. 'You know, we've five people under twenty years. About 60 per cent are under forty years, the rest are old. That's not bad. But even for us, it's ending. The younger generation don't want to learn Torah and our boys rarely go to synagogue. Ours is a dispersed community now. In the past there was pressure to observe. People watched. "Who's missing synagogue? Why?"'

Even in Babu's day, the choice of brides was limited and in the end he defied his 'militant' mother by marrying a woman from the Bene Israel Jews in Mumbai. As the father of two daughters, the headache is much worse now. But unlike his mother, Babu had no plans to bully his children to conform.

'I see an even worse problem for my daughters,' he said. 'My elder daughter doesn't want to stay.'

'What does she want to do?'

'Oh, she dreams of NASA, the space mission. She's brilliant at science: 99 per cent for maths, 98 per cent for physics, 97 per cent for chemistry. She'll go if she gets the chance. The younger one is totally the opposite. She's relaxed. She doesn't worry about her future, a job, a husband. One wants to go to the very top, be the first. The second says, "Papa, I don't mind being last, as long as I am happy."' He laughed and patted his moustaches with evident pride at the thought of them both.

'But I wish for them a good husband, from good family, with good job. Such a man is more important than any Black or White Jewish thing. Now there're no Jews here for them to marry, so what to do? We have to look to the Jews elsewhere. Bring new blood back to Cochin. We have to make our choice. Or be like the others and simply die.'

*

The next day was the first night of Shmini, followed by Simhat Torah, when the community celebrated the end of the yearly cycle of reading their holy book. Also, falling on a Friday, it would coincide with preparations for Sabbath.

Babu asked me to join him and his wife for lunch on Friday. Then in the evening I was invited to come to their prayer service at their other synagogue in Ernakulam,

Kadavunbagam, and join the celebratory meal afterwards. After the cold reception I had received from the most senior elder of the White Jews, I was touched. I accepted.

I arrived at Babu's home the next day at lunchtime. It was a small, square, whitewashed house, with a gateway and path to the side leading to the main entrance and hallway. The first door on the left opened into a bedroom, while a second led into the living and dining room. The kitchen was at the back of the house and was abuzz with activity, the steam and heat of cooking and the clatter of pots and pans sending tantalizing wafts of curry through the house. The dining room was painted a cool blue, the open windows on either side allowing a pleasant cross breeze.

I sat at the large dining table and was given a glass of pulped grape juice by Ofra. She was a pretty woman in her forties, with black hair tied in a bun, warm brown eyes and a rounded frame. Her marriage to Babu had been a love match. Babu saw her at the synagogue in Bombay and was taken immediately. She was a diligent wife and mother, rising every day at five for prayers and then preparing the children's breakfasts and meals and packing the youngest one off to pre-school by 6.30. The oldest one was studying at college some three hours' distance away and came back at weekends to see the family. Ofra's duties also involved assisting the Ernakulam Jewish community.

That morning had been particularly frantic and she looked exhausted. Her forehead shone with sweat and her forearms were damp with the exertion of beating the sundown deadline.

Ofra and the servant were busy preparing snacks for the dinner at the synagogue, the three meals for Sabbath and the Simhat Torah festival, which would be shared with the Muslim servants, plus lunch for all of us today. The young Muslim assistants from the aquarium had popped by as Babu had told them to get their lunch at his house that day. The boys leaned against the wall, drinking juice as they joked with the lady of the house while waiting for their meal. The mood was light and affectionate and they seemed more like Ofra's sons than her husband's employees; there was nothing to indicate that one was a Jew and the others Muslim.

The Sabbath meals were hot and ready in great aluminium cooking pots. As the servants prepared to leave, Ofra hunched low and ladled portions into tiffin cans for them to carry home to their families. 'Since it's festival, we share our food with them,' she explained. 'For many years we couldn't afford it because of the children, but now they're older we like to do this again,' she said.

Having fed the boys, she turned her attention to making pastries to take to the party that evening. She was making a classic Kerala Jewish festival snack called *pastels*, with shredded chicken, fried with ginger, pepper, grated carrot, onions, cabbage and boiled eggs. She stood at the dining table, chatting airily as she mixed the filling with one hand, while with the other she kneaded the dough that would be used for the pastry cases. She rolled the dough out and cut out round circles. She placed a spoonful of mixture in each and then sealed it. The frilled semi-circles would then be deep fried.

'We'll take this to the synagogue tonight,' she explained. 'Tonight almost all of the Ernakulam Jews will come for prayers. You'll see.'

The Paradesi Synagogue was the only one that remained in proper service, with the other seven almost permanently out of use. So, on the days of major festivals, everyone would gather in Mattancheri for prayers, some making a journey of almost two hours to get there. That morning the Ernakulam Jews had gone early to the Paradesi Synagogue for the first prayer service of the Shmini and Simchat Torah weekend. This evening, prior to sundown, they would honour the old tradition of lighting the candles on a metal tree to mark the festival of Shmini, followed by prayers at 7.30, after which the Jews could invite special guests to the synagogue and view the decorations. Prayers would continue on Saturday morning and evening and then again into Sunday. The new Torah cycle began the following week.

'Every Jewish community celebrates Simhat Torah in its own way. In Bombay you'll see them celebrate it with great joy,' said Ofra, nostalgic for her old city. 'There you'll see the real happiness, the dancing and singing. Tradition tells us to take the Torah and dance.' She twirled in a circle, her flour-covered forearms lifted high in a moment of lightness.

Ofra noted with amusement that not much dancing could be seen in Cochin these days, as the Jews were mostly too elderly and weak to carry the heavy scrolls. In the old days, strapping men from the community would carry the heavy scrolls in their cases and literally cavort around the courtyard,

leaping high and dancing as the other Jews followed behind singing and clapping. Grainy black-and-white photos from the heyday show a riotous celebration of the holy book, with worshippers high on bottles of spirits known as 'petrol'. Bottles of 'petrol' were swigged early in the morning before going to synagogue, and it was not unknown for some to secrete their own supply in the courtyard itself to fortify themselves during the drawn-out prayers and proceedings. Tomorrow the Jews would dance with one symbolic Torah, but I imagined at their age it would be more of a stately waltz.

With the *pastels* prepared, Ofra cleared the table and set it for lunch. Babu was back from the aquarium. His wife laid down an array of dishes as if by magic: chicken curry with the tiny sweet potatoes I had seen in the market, rice, a special dish of diced chicken pieces fried in a masala batter, salad and homemade pickle. The two recalled how, when they first married, it had taken a while for Ofra to adjust to the change of pace from Bombay. At first she found it tough. After all, Bombay was this fast, cosmopolitan city, home to business and Bollywood as well as lords of the criminal underworld, a world of glamour and danger embraced within a glittering emerald bay.

Cochin was unhurried, provincial, a place where the idea of a night out was an evening of bridge with the elders. The tight-knit community that knew everybody's business, the suppurating humidity of the wet lowlands made for a claustrophobic existence. Babu was still amused when he

recalled Ofra's shock at leaving her 'big Bombay life'.

'Why stay, why not migrate to Israel?' I asked.

'I did go, just to see,' he replied evenly. 'I stayed there for a month or so to see if we could live there. But I decided we couldn't.'

'Why?'

'I hated it,' he said simply. 'I found the Israelis arrogant. There's no love in their hearts for people like us. Here in India, the Malabari Jews are loved by all parts of the community. There I felt like the outsider. Maybe it's because of the way they live – modern society, too fast, no time for tradition, the synagogue, community. There it's work, spend, eat, sleep. *Bus*. They're closed in mind, closed in heart. Perhaps because of the troubles they face. The political troubles, I mean. Enemies on each side. Living in siege. Always fearing the outsider, the dark face. I couldn't let my family live like this – fearing what might happen.'

The sacrifice would have been too much. The Jews of Kerala had never known the persecution, the fear that other Diaspora communities faced. The Ernakulam Jews, in particular, were close to the Hindus, Muslims and Christians. Babu was mindful of just how much he had to lose.

'Here in India, in Kerala, we're accepted. We're safe. Why change this? When I got on the plane to leave Israel, even though it's my Holy Land, I was happy to be coming home. You know that smell when you step off the plane in India? That dirty diesel smell!' Tears welled in his eyes as he smiled. 'I can't tell you how happy I was to breathe my country into

my lungs. I'm Jewish. But I'm also Indian. What's Israel to me? It's a foreign country.'

Then why did the Black Jews not share the despair of the White Jews, despite knowing that this was the end for them too?

'They're all old now, their youngsters are gone. Who's left to make them happy? All their lives, they wanted to be exclusive. Now they have their wish. They're excluded from everything.'

The Malabari Jews, Babu said, had always been closer to the Indian mentality. 'Throughout history we mixed with the other communities, we're part of them, they're part of us. We belong here still. There's life here still. Plus, we have young children with us. Only problem – who will they marry?'

'Will your girls go to Israel to find a husband?'

'The older daughter only has NASA space station on her mind. Not Cochin, the universe! The younger one is happy to stay here for ever. What's for them in Israel? My sister was one of those who made the aliyah, the pilgrimage to Israel. She wanted a new life, a new beginning. She went many years ago, married an Israeli and they had four children there.'

'How does she like it?'

'My sister's now divorced. Her husband left them. That is their way there. That is *her* Israel,' he said, the hard edge discernible in his voice again.

Then, without warning, Babu began to weep, cupping his right hand over his eyes as tears rolled down his cheeks into his food. Ofra placed her hand on his arm in silent reassurance.

I sensed Babu was crying for more than his sister's sadness. Eventually the tears stopped and he smiled, as if embarrassed by such foolishness. He wiped his eyes with the back of his hand and began eating again, his right hand kneading the rice into a neat ball as he continued the meal in silence.

For Babu, Israel had not been the Promised Land. He was one of many who went there with expectations of finding a sense of belonging after a history of rejection by the White Jews in India. But his *aliyah* provided neither the answers nor the acceptance craved by those Black Jews who left. Instead he discovered an Israel torn asunder by religious insecurity, a land where peace was a stranger still. For his sister, and even for himself on that one brief trip, Israel was not the fabled paradise that held them spellbound in childhood, but a void of loneliness and rejection. India, for all its failings, remained home.

Five

Land of Black Gold and White Pearls

*'What strange tales would history unfold if the gift of
speech was allowed to the stones and pebbles that lie
embedded in the bosom of the river that flows by the once
famous Cranganore?'*

K. P. P. Menon, *History of Kerala*

From the inception of their community on the shores of
Malabar two thousand or more years ago, the Cochini Jews
never forgot they were the people of Israel and that this was
only an interim homeland. Israel was invoked in prayer
almost daily, toasted at festivals with the best whisky or
arrack, a toddy made with cashews. The court of Solomon,
the fall of the Second Temple and Jerusalem some one
thousand years later and the resulting forced migration were
not merely the stuff of antiquity but part of their identity.
Babu's tears did not spring from sentimentality – he was a
tough and pragmatic man, after all – but originated in
a profound sense of rejection, akin to a long-lost son

finding no instinctive embrace from a father on his return.

Understanding the White Jews' history is part of deciphering who they are. The ten windows of the Paradesi Synagogue represented the ten commandments, the two pillars flanking the Ark were inspired by the destroyed Temple of Solomon, the hangings adorning the synagogue walls shared the sacred colours used in the ancient holy of holies. Each detail, down to the last carved flower, was a reminder of a lost Jerusalem. The synagogue was a manifestation of faith to replace Israel until it was recovered. When the Black Jews were barred from worship in the Paradesi Synagogue, it echoed the darkness and estrangement of the past.

*

It was during the golden days of King Solomon's rule that the first contact was made between Israel and India. By the time Solomon took the throne in 970 BCE, he had inherited from his father David a significant regional empire. Jerusalem was no longer a minor city-cum-state but the capital of this empire. To mark its ascendancy in status and power, Solomon embarked upon an ambitious building programme which included a royal acropolis near Mount Zion, a palace and other grand architectural statements such as the House of the Forest of Lebanon. There was a treasury and the Judgment Hall, which housed Solomon's ivory throne, as well as a separate palatial residence for his most politically important and illustrious wife, the daughter of the pharaoh.

But the most significant building of all was the Temple to Yahweh, which came to be known as the Temple of Solomon. No physical trace of this first temple survives its destruction by the King of Babylon, Nebuchadnezzar, in 586 BCE, but it lives on almost three millennia later through biblical accounts which describe it in minute detail. It remains ever present in the spiritual landscape of the Jewish people, symbolizing an era in their history when God dwelled among them in the house that Solomon built.

The Temple of Solomon contained the Ark of the Covenant, a chest which held the tablets of Law handed down to Moses. Mounted upon the Ark were two golden cherubim whose wings fanned outwards to form a throne for Yahweh. This throne symbolized the presence of the divine among his people, an indication that Yahweh himself sat in the midst of his worshippers. Responsibility for carrying the Ark had always been in the hands of the tribe of Levi, a caste of priests of whom Moses' brother, Aaron, was chief. Its stewardship was of the highest importance and its care entrusted to a select few. The Ark was believed to have a terrible sacred power which would protect the Jewish people against their enemies, helping to smite them in battle.

The Ark was the only symbol of the divine presence in the Temple, which contained no effigies; when God appeared to Moses in the burning bush, he declared he must not be defined by any human form. While the Ark remained in the Temple, it was seen by the Jewish people as a spiritual epicentre that directly connected mortal life to heaven, to God himself.

The Temple itself conformed to the typical imperial architecture of the region. In the courtyard in front of the Temple stood an altar of sacrifice as well as a huge bronze basin representing Yam, the primal sea. This alluded to the forces of darkness or chaos, a reminder of how the Jewish people had escaped slavery in Egypt.

The main temple entrance was flanked by the pillars and its walls, both inside and out, were etched with angels and cherubs, almonds and flowers and swaying palm trees. A central staircase led up to the main *Ulam*, or vestibule, which in turn led through to the *Hekhal*, or cult hall, at the eastern end of the building. Another flight of stairs separated this chamber from the *Devir*, or Holy of Holies, which contained the Ark itself, screened from view by a curtain of blue, crimson and purple. These same colours are seen in the Paradesi Synagogue's central chamber.

One cannot over-emphasize the significance of the Temple of Solomon to the faithful, then as well as now. The Temple, abode of Yahweh himself, was the sanctuary of one's faith. Solomon was also seen as a special king, for God had granted him the honour of building a Temple in his name. The king of the Jews was a ruler anointed by God: his palace resided next to the house of God; his seat of power was beside Yahweh's own throne on the Ark. In *A History of Jerusalem* Karen Armstrong describes the duty of the leader of the Jewish people to impart justice:

If this justice prevailed there would be peace, harmony

and fertility in the kingdom. Yahweh would provide them with the security which was so earnestly and continually sought for in the ancient world... But there was no security and no shalom if there was no justice in Zion.

Shalom meant more than just peace, it signified a spiritual wholeness and harmony with the world. Maybe this link between justice and shalom explains why the latter-day Jews of Cochin felt retribution had befallen their own kingdom in India. The history of the Jews of Kerala shows that justice did not always prevail.

While Solomon was revered for his wisdom and for giving the Jewish people the first temple, in the end justice and shalom evaded his kingdom. The heavy cost of his building programme was a drain on national resources and required large-scale conscripted labour. As Solomon built his glittering new Jerusalem, the demand grew for luxuries with which to furnish it. This opened up an era of sea-faring voyages from Israel to India as Solomon's men sought out exotic treasures to bring back to his kingdom.

In *The Last Jews of Cochin: Jewish Identity in Hindu India*, Nathan Katz and Ellen Goldberg note that the Hebrew Bible contained a number of words which were very similar to Sanskrit and Tamil, suggesting there were well-established links between Solomon's kingdom and India. The *First Book of Kings* indicates that the opulence of the court of King Solomon was partly attributable to this trade.

Other historians also flagged up these biblical clues. In

The Jews of Kerala, P. M. Jussay suggests that the earliest Jews were sailors from King Solomon's ships, which, according to the Bible, brought 'once every three years, silver, elephant's tooth, peacocks and apes'. He points out that the Bible's word for peacock is *tukiyum* and for apes it is *kapim*. The Tamil words for peacock and ape are *tokai* and *kapi*. The ancient Roman chronicles of Pliny the Elder including *The Periplus of the Erythraean Sea* also provide evidence of maritime trade between the Red Sea coast and Muziris, another name for Cranganore.

So began the first contact between the two countries, as trading partners. According to the verbal history of the Jews of Cochin, some of these first merchant traders and their slaves may have settled on the coast of Kerala. Historians believe the Jews who arrived on the trading ships were unlikely to have travelled with their families. Local rulers would have provided these foreign customers with lodging, and the Jews would have had relationships with local women. The resulting children founded the Jewish community in Kerala.

A further trickle of settlers came to India several centuries after Solomon's rule, at the time of the destruction of the first temple in 586 BCE by the Babylonian ruler Nebuchadnezzar. In a merciless assault, Jerusalem was sacked and the Temple of Solomon was gutted of its precious furnishings and burned to the ground. The contents of the temple were taken to Babylon, but the fate of the Ark was not recorded. It simply vanished from history. The disappearance of the seat of Yahweh was interpreted as a sign that God had deserted the

Jewish people. The Jewish people were exiles, with many having to protect their faith in Babylon, the land of their new master. Others reportedly fled to far-flung lands, including India.

The loss of the temple was shattering. The earthly seat of God had been razed, the holy kingdom transformed into a wasteland and the people scattered. There was no longer a physical manifestation of the spiritual epicentre of their faith. The link between heaven and earth had been severed.

But the hope of returning and rebuilding their Jerusalem was not extinguished. Instead, in their period of banishment, these first exiles sought to preserve the purity of their faith: keeping the Sabbath, circumcising their male children, and so on. They remained separate from non-Jews. These were the outwards signs of the Jews being a holy people. By refusing to relinquish their faith and maintaining their separateness, the hope of return to Israel was kept alive and eventually realized by some. This was the mentality adopted by the Cochin Jews during their time in India.

By 520 BCE the foundations of the Second Temple in Jerusalem had been laid and on the Jewish feast of Sukkoth a special dedication ceremony was held by the priests. This new building lacked the magnificence of the Temple of Solomon and it no longer housed the sacred Ark, but it did resurrect hope. Some 500 years later, in 19 BCE, Herod decided to fully restore the Second Temple, returning it to something approaching the resplendence of the first. To ensure the holy site was not polluted by ordinary men, he had a thousand priests

trained as masons and carpenters so that they could take responsibility for the *Hekhal* and *Devir*. So the new temple was completed.

The Second Temple drew huge numbers of pilgrims. During Herod's rule, as many as half a million came to the major feast days such as Passover and Sukkoth. The atmosphere at these times was one of enormous jubilation. On the special festival of Sukkoth, or Tabernacles, which marks the Israelites' period in the desert after their Exodus from Egypt, each Jewish family would prepare a sacrificial lamb at the Temple. The ecstasy of return after exile, of seeing their temple resurrected to its former glory, was a remarkable reversal of fortune for the Jewish people.

But it did not last. By 70 CE the Jews were crushed once again. In that year the Romans laid siege to Jerusalem and broke into the Temple's inner courts. Six thousand Jewish zealots lay in wait, willing to lay down their lives to defend their beloved Temple. Even in the face of death, they were careful to safeguard the purity laws associated with the Temple chambers. The second-century Greek historian Dio Cassius describes the incredible fortitude of the Jewish faithful: 'The ordinary people fought in the forecourt and the nobility in the inner courts while the priests defended the Temple building itself.' It was to no avail and when the Jews saw the Second Temple ablaze, they uttered cries of despair, with some of those present throwing themselves upon the sword of the enemy or plunging into the flames rather than live to see their Temple destroyed.

The Temple was smashed to pieces by Roman troops and only the Western Wall of the *Devir* remained standing. The wall is all that survives and it is the most sacred place for Jews around the world. Even now, the memory of the Temple's destruction has the power to move its people to tears. When I visited the Western Wall, or Wailing Wall as it is also known, the reawakened sorrow and despair were palpable: people would come to the wall to pray and then, without warning, their bodies would crumple, fingertips clinging on to the pale yellow brickwork as they wept into the stones.

The Jewish people were left in no doubt about their position after the fall of Jerusalem and the Temple. After 70 CE there was a Roman coin in circulation that depicted a Jewess with hands bound tight as she sat under a palm tree. An order was issued to the Romans to hunt down and execute any Jew who claimed to descend from King David. Jewish property was confiscated and many were driven out. The people faced humiliation and a kind of religious emasculation in their own city. The temple taxes extracted from male Jews by the Romans were donated to the Temple of Jupiter in Rome. Roman soldiers would make sacrifices to their gods in Jerusalem's streets. The Jewish holy city was defiled and the remains of the Temple were polluted by the blood of its own people.

Even decades after the destruction, the Jewish people remained in a state of shock and spiritual paralysis. The *Book of Baruch* says that nature itself should succumb to a period of mourning:

For why should light rise again
Where the light of Zion is darkened?

In the period after the fall of Jerusalem, Jews were again expelled from their holy city; again, they were exiles. At this juncture in history the first large community of Jewish migrants came from Israel to India. Trading links with Kerala went back almost a millennium; now the Jews of Israel came not as merchant traders, but as refugees. How could they know it would be millennia before they returned? This pivotal moment in Cochini Jewish history provides the link between the sacred city and what would become a substitute Jerusalem in India, the port city of Cranganore. Out of the fire and devastation of Jerusalem, thus a community of Jews was delivered on the west coast of Kerala.

*

That India should have been a natural choice of refuge for the Jews during this tumultuous period is explained by various factors. As we have seen, trade was well established between Israel and India from the time of Solomon, but this was given fresh impetus by 45 CE with the discovery by Hippalus of the monsoon winds, which cut the sea journey to India dramatically.

The Indian community was well looked upon in Jewish society, it would appear. Josephus describes in his chronicles that in Israel during the time of the destruction of the Second

Temple, there was some knowledge of Hindu philosophy. According to Katz and Goldberg, in Josephus' account of the mass martyrdom of Masada in 73 CE the leader of the Jewish zealots, Eleazar, referred to Hindu philosophy towards death during his battle cry to his followers. Masada is renowned in Jewish history as the last stand against the Romans. Nearly 1,000 Jews held out against the attackers in the mountain-top fortress overlooking the Dead Sea. When the Romans finally breached the defences, they found a scene of mass slaughter: the entire community had committed suicide rather than surrender to the enemy. In Hinduism, death is seen as part of the ongoing cycle of destruction and rebirth. Eleazar had drawn upon this to persuade his followers to embrace martyrdom:

> We... ought to become an example to others of our readiness to die. Yet if we do stand in need of foreigners to support us in this matter, let us regard those Indians... These have such a desire of a life of immortality that they tell other men beforehand that they are about to depart and nobody hinders them but every one thinks them happy men...

Josephus said the Masada Jews were swayed by Eleazar's argument and decided to make the ultimate sacrifice to protect the honour of their faith. The writer William Whitson concurs with the theory that Hindu beliefs had permeated early Jewish culture: 'How was there knowledge of Indian beliefs and practices? Josephus is described by some scholars as a

Hellenized Jew with knowledge of Greek historians who held Indian philosophy in high regard.'

So Hindu culture was already part of Jewish consciousness and, in turn, the Keralites welcomed foreigners to their shores, seeing them as a source of revenue and skills which enhanced the regional economy.

By this time, the Romans had established a colony at Muziris on the Malabar coast. In 60 CE, Pliny the Elder described the scene in *The Periplus of the Erythraean Sea*, a mariners' guide to the Red Sea and Indian Ocean: 'Muziris... abounds in ships sent there with cargoes from Arabia and by the Greeks... Kings send large ships to those market towns on account of the great quantity and bulk of pepper.'

Ships came loaded with gold and returned with holds bursting with black pepper. Such exchanges ensured that Muziris consolidated its position as a wealthy port city and cosmopolitan hub with a rather raffish air. The great classical second-century Tamil poem the *Shilappadikaram*, or *Lay of the Ankle Bracelet*, portrays a city glinting with foreign gold, where 'lusty sailors sang' and 'all night, lamps were burning, the lamps of foreigners who talk strange tongues, who watch over precious cargoes near the docks'.

Against this energizing backdrop of fast-expanding trade and migration from Israel, Greece, Syria and Rome, Jews arrived to establish their first large-scale settlement in Kerala. The earliest Jewish settlements were in Calicut and Quilon, but the most important of all was Cranganore. The Jews settled on the northern side of Cranganore at Pullot, where

there was a ferry service beside the temple to cross the water. The word 'ferry' in Malayalam is *kadavu* and so the Jewish settlement came to be known as Kadavumbagam, or 'the ferry side'. The Jewish settlement on the southern bank of the river Periyar was known as Tekkumbagam; these communities were made up of poorer Jews who were involved in the docks or as commercial agents.

There was also a settlement at Cherigandaram of Jewish merchants. It was in this area that Joseph Rabban settled after the raja conferred princely privileges on him. These rights, sometimes described as the Cochini Jews' Magna Carta, were set out on the engraved copper plates which now lie in the Paradesi Synagogue. They were awarded to the Jews as a result of the Chera-Chola conflict, which was being fought in the south around 1000 CE. During a crisis in the long-running war, the Chera king, Bhaskara Ravi Varma, convened a war council. It is believed that Rabban agreed to help him, placing assets and men at his disposal, and so the king raised the status of the Jewish settlement to an autonomous entity and made Rabban the head, granting the seventy-two privileges. Rabin's reward for such fealty was a kingdom of his own, in perpetuity.

Cochin's line of Hindu kings would honour the deal struck with Rabban and the Jews were held in extremely high regard, even centuries later. According to numerous historical accounts, this close relationship between the Jews and the raja of the princely state is unique within India. The Jews in the Indian cities of Bombay and Calcutta were successful

businessmen but did not have the same political privileges bestowed by the local ruling power.

Until Independence in 1947 the Jews benefited from a number of privileges in Cochin, which remained a Hindu princely state until the British left India. For example, Jewish holidays were observed and the banks were closed on Rosh Hashanah and Yom Kippur. Exams were never held for Jewish students on Shabbat and they were given a seat on the legislative council of the state of Cochin, even though they did not have a big enough population to justify this. Jews were also allocated a certain number of places at medical and law school.

Today, where Cranganore once stood there is little trace of its momentous history. Most of the ancient city was destroyed in periodic attacks by Arab and Portuguese soldiers, but it is evoked in the second-century Tamil epic poem *Mani-mekalai*, or *Dancer with Magic Bowl*, which describes a city 'surrounded by a moat': 'On the surface of the water floated large lotus flowers, red and white water lilies and the blue iris.' The residential quarters were graced with 'wide avenues' where guards watched over 'rich dwellings'. There were parks with trees and flowers and 'pools with such limpid water that the inhabitants of heaven left their paradise to visit these banks'.

In his *History of Kerala*, K. P. P. Menon marvels at the importance of Cranganore in world history. It was here that Solomon's ships alighted; here that St Thomas first arrived in India in 52 CE, planted a cross and preached Christianity,

according to Kerala tradition; here that numerous trading powers, from the Chinese and Arabs to the Portuguese and Dutch, arrived with lofty ambitions of conquest and commerce. Today, its crumbling ruins are the abode of howling jackals. 'The old moat is the haunt of crocodiles and paddy birds,' Menon lamented.

One of the earliest Jewish accounts of Malabar was written by the merchant Benjamin of Tudela, who chronicled the life of Jewish communities across the world. He described the stupefying heat of an Indian summer:

> From Passover to New Year... no man can go out of his house because of the sun, for the heat in that country is intense. Everybody remains in his house until the evening. They go forth and kindle lights in all the market places and all the street and do their work and business at night-time. For they have to turn night into day in consequence of the great heat of the sun.

Turning to the Jewish community of Malabar in particular, he describes 'only about one hundred Jews who were of Black colour as well as the other inhabitants. The Jews are good men, observers of the law and possess the Pentateuch; the people have some little knowledge of the Talmud.'

Further impressions are provided by the 'Cairo Genizah documents', a collection of 250,000 documents once stored in the anteroom of a synagogue in Old Cairo. *Genizah* means 'hiding place' in Hebrew. When the archive was discovered in

1896, there were documents spanning several hundred years that give an insight into Jewish life in the Middle Ages, including missives written by Jewish merchants who started to travel between the Mediterranean and China in the ninth century, stopping along Malabar's coast.

Translated by Solomon D. Goitein, the letters painted a vivid picture of India: of the homesickness of the traders who missed family life, how they savoured the kosher cheeses sent as a gift from their wives in Alexandria and Aden; how the men lapsed into using concubines during their long leaves of absence. The archive is a window into the lives of Jewish antiquity. For example, some seventy fragments portray the life of a Tunisian-born Jew called Abraham Ben Yiju. He set off to make his fortune in trade with India in the 1120s. The documents depict the small triumphs and tragedies that make up a lifetime. His correspondence tells of a difficult journey, his business dealings and marriage to an Indian slave girl called Ashu; his acumen in the import-export business – he exported iron and spices to his Jewish partners in Aden while importing arsenic, paper and other commodities to India; the birth of his three children and then the premature death of his young son in India.

Ben Yiju's letters tell one of the most important stories of the Jews who migrated to and worked in India. He was a highly educated merchant, noted for his scholarship and calligraphy. His correspondence with Aden illustrates the type of trade that existed with India at the time. There is some suggestion that he also traded slaves. He opened a brass

factory on the Malabar coast at one point, which employed local Jews as well as others.

Clearly, he was well regarded by his business partners. One letter from a trading associate in Aden acknowledging a shipment of black pepper concludes with the following gushing sentiments: 'The letter of my lord, the most illustrious elder, has arrived; may God make permanent your well being, may he guard your life and humble those who envy you.'

After spending some eighteen years in India, Ben Yiju left in 1149 to return to Aden, only to find many of his family had left the country. He received a frosty reception from the Jewish community, who questioned the validity of his marriage. His homecoming was a less than happy one.

Marco Polo also travelled to the region during the late thirteenth century and his travelogue mentions the kingdom of what is now Quilon on Malabar's coast:

> It is the residence of many Christians and Jews, who retain their proper language. The king is not a tributary to any other... The heat during some months is so violent as to be scarcely supportable; yet the merchants resort thither from various parts of the world... attracted by great profits.

Cranganore was famous not just for commodities but for precious stones such as diamonds, rubies and pearls. As early as Roman times they were in much demand. In his chronicle *Naturalis Historia*, the Roman military commander, philosopher and writer, Pliny the Elder, made clear his disapproval of

the appetite for such fripperies from what he called 'India's first emporium':

> Our ladies glory in having pearls suspended from their fingers, one, two or three of them dangling from their ears, delighted even with the rattling of pearls as they knock against each other; and now, the poorer classes are even affecting them as people are in the habit of saying 'a pearl worn by a woman in public is as good as a lector walking before her'.

Pliny was equally disapproving of the insatiable appetite for black pepper among his countrymen, clearly fearing it would bleed Rome's coffers dry: 'Both pepper and ginger grow wild... and yet we buy them by weight like silver and gold,' he sniffed.

Nose-tickling bounties of pepper, known as 'black gold'; exquisite shawls and turbans embellished with silver thread; luminescent pearls and corals harvested from the sea bed; perfumed camphor and oils destined to grace the boudoir of some fragrant foreign matron. These were the treasures that drove men from the sanctuary of family life to perilous sea voyages, leading them to the heat-induced madness of Malabar summers and into the arms of their velvet-eyed lovers.

Such was the scene at a time when Cranganore was the most important of cities in the region. As we have seen, the city was not just a trading centre but a place imbued with religious significance. What would drive the Jews from such a place?

The old Shingly songs, the musical history of the people, hinted at quarrels over funds for the synagogue that led to a rupture in the Jewish leadership. But in 1341, it was nature not man that decided the fate of the Cranganore Jews. As a result of a torrential downpour, the river Periyar flooded, silting up the harbour mouth. Because of this biblical-style flood, Cranganore lost its strategic maritime position. A new harbour formed at Cochin, which was smaller but would replace Cranganore as the regional port. It was called Kochazhi, or 'small estuary', and eventually became known as Kochi or Cochin.

Faced with this natural disaster, the first party of Jews left for Cochin. The Jews settled in swiftly. Indeed, by 1345 a synagogue was built there. It was known as the Kochangadi Synagogue and was the first outside Cranganore. As Cochin's importance rose in the region, so Cranganore's declined. The Jews who remained in the old city over the next two centuries found their power and influence diminish as trade switched to Cochin. The kingdom of Cochin, under the raja, found itself at loggerheads with the local dominant power at Calicut in the north, whose rulers were known as the Zamorins.

It was the Zamorins who first had contact with the Portuguese with the arrival of Vasco da Gama in the fifteenth century. At the time the Arabs dominated this lucrative trade route and the Portuguese were keen to take over. In Gaspar Correa's *Three Voyages*, which describes the Portuguese assault on the Malabar Coast, there is a fascinating description of da Gama's first encounter with the ruler of Zamorin at

Calicut. Da Gama looked every inch the European dandy when he was received at the royal court, dressed:

> in a long cloak, coming down to his feet, of tawny-coloured satin, lined with smooth brocade, and underneath a short tunic of blue satin and white buskins, and on his head a cap of blue velvet with a white feather fastened with a splendid medal; and a valuable enamel collar on his shoulders and a rich sash with a handsome dagger.

The king received him 'seated on a rich bed set out with silk and gold', wearing bracelets studded with jewels, including a diamond as thick as his thumb. Around his neck were pearls 'the size of hazelnuts' and a necklace of rubies and emeralds.

Da Gama wanted to secure a trade agreement, but the king was non-committal. Relations deteriorated when the Portuguese were asked to pay customs duty to the port where their ships were docked before departing. Da Gama refused and simply left. He returned to Portugal to report his findings and was hailed as a hero for discovering the sea route. He had come bearing goods worth 60 times the cost of the voyage, so plans were made for an armada of thirty-three ships to return. This time the person in charge was Pedro Alvarez Cabral, a man of 'overweening pride' who perceived insults in every innocent gesture and had 'neither tact nor foresight', according to *Malabar and the Portuguese* by K. M. Panikkar. On arrival, Cabral made the fundamental error of sending a low-born fisherman to give a message to the sovereign, which was

interpreted as a great insult in caste-based India. The Portuguese finally got permission to build a factory in Calicut, but the rocky start boded ill.

The Portuguese believed they now had the right to the trade route and saw themselves as lords of the seas, with the right to confiscate goods of those who sailed in the region without their permission. Cabral seized an Arab ship in harbour because it was loading pepper he wanted for himself. He did not believe natives had the right to sell to whoever paid the best price. The news angered the locals, unused to such aggressive tactics. A riot ensued and the factory was destroyed and many Portuguese were wounded.

The Portuguese responded by massacring the crew of all other boats and burning their ships. The rulers decided the Portuguese were 'uncivilized barbarians, treacherous, untrustworthy'. The Zamorin and Portuguese were now enemies. Cabral was advised by a Jew-turned-Christian in his crew, Gaspar da India, that he should sail to Cochin. He reached there on Christmas Eve in 1500. There he sought an audience with the local raja. A treaty was drawn up and he was granted permission to buy all he wished and to build another factory. At that time the raja of Cochin was fearful of the powerful Zamorin and saw the Portuguese as potential allies in his bid for autonomy. In the end, the raja simply exchanged one bondage for another as the Portuguese governor assumed the position of colonial overlord. The Portuguese built garrisons at their new base, as well as more factories. But their old enemy plagued their ambitions for expansion.

The rulers of Calicut wanted vengeance on the foreign invader and in the years that followed they waged a war with the Portuguese and their new ally, the raja of Cochin. Once the Jews moved from Cranganore to Cochin, they too would be embroiled in this bloody feud.

The Zamorins, together with their allies the Arabs, also wanted to expand their territory beyond Calicut, leading to clashes with the Jews of Cranganore as well as the Portuguese. In 1524 the feuding between the Jews and Arabs of Cranganore reached a flashpoint when a row broke out over the adulteration of the supply of pepper, which led to the death of a Muslim. Angry and looking for a fight, the Muslims attacked the Jews, killing some of their number, burning their houses and synagogues. The Calicut rulers gave their blessing to the attack.

It was too much for the remaining Jews of Cranganore to bear and another wave migrated to Cochin. The Jewish people were now scattered across numerous communities in Cochin. Having lost the old settlement given to them centuries earlier, they were given sanctuary by the Hindu raja of Cochin, who allotted them parcels of land that would become known as the Jew Towns of Mattancheri and Ernakulam.

By the seventeenth century there were synagogues across Ernakulam and Cochin. The Malabari Jews named the new synagogues after those in Cranganore in order to keep tradition alive. While Cochin was to become forever associated with the Jewry of the region, Cranganore remained their spiritual homeland in India. The very last of the Jews had left Cranganore

around 1566. By this time the Portuguese were well established on the western coast and in Cochin, with ambitions to turn it into the most important trading port of the region. From 1503 to 1663 the Portuguese were the dominant foreign power in Cochin, where the raja remained a titular head. The Portuguese turned out to be cruel overlords, persecuting the Jewish people until the Dutch displaced them.

It was in the sixteenth century that the final major wave of Jewish immigrants came from overseas to join the older communities from Cranganore. The newcomers were escaping the horrors of the Inquisition in Europe. In her essay 'The Cochin Jews of Kerala', the historian Barbara Johnson says that some were Sephardic Jews, refugees from the Spanish and Portuguese expulsions. Others came via Constantinople, Aleppo and other Middle Eastern territories.

Some of this wave of refugees came as families, but the single men among them married some of the Jewish women from the so-called first families of Cranganore. In 1568 the newcomers built a synagogue on the plot of land next to the raja's palace in Cochin. Johnson writes in her essay:

> They adopted the Malayalam language and identified enthusiastically with Kerala customs and traditions, but at some point they stopped marrying the Jews who had been there many centuries before them. In written accounts, the Paradesis were referred to as 'White Jews' and the more ancient Malabari communities as 'Black Jews', though there is not

always a clear distinction between them in terms of skin colour.

In the early years of Cochini life, the two communities came together and in some cases intermarried. Fleeing the brutality and persecution of the Inquisition in Europe, the Paradesi Jews quickly assimilated into life in India. Unlike Jews elsewhere in the world, they found acceptance among the natives and the existing Jewish community. It started with promise, so what changed to create a fissure that would take centuries to repair?

*

As a community, the Jews had to tiptoe through the minefield of colonial rivalries for ascendancy in the region. In 1662 the Jews united with the Dutch against the hated Portuguese, who had targeted them mercilessly. During their time on India's west coast, the Portuguese used force to convert locals to Christianity and even introduced the Inquisition in neighbouring Goa in the early sixteenth century. Goa would eventually become the Portuguese epicentre for trade.

The Jews of Cochin found themselves in the firing line for their faith and allegiance to the Dutch in 1662. The Portuguese exacted their revenge by burning the synagogue, Torah scrolls and records and then sacked Jew Town. But by 1663 the Dutch had defeated the Portuguese, opening up a period of benign colonial relations for the Jews, who enjoyed a

renaissance of culture and trade. Cochin grew more prosperous and the Jews reaped the benefits of links with the rest of the Dutch empire through shipments of books and contact with Jewish communities in Europe.

The first British troops came to Malabar in 1615 but did not replace the Dutch as the dominant colonial power in Cochin until 1797. The British presence was confined to Fort Cochin and Willingdon Island.

In the centuries that followed the Jews' move to Cochin, they had to play a canny game, not just to survive as a minority community but also to exploit Cochin's significance on the world trading map. Their key advantage was the strong historic links to the royal family. In the days of Joseph Rabban, Jews had established close ties with the raja and joined his men in battle. The Cochini royal family never forgot the favour. The Jews lived on plots of land provided by the royal family and the Paradesi Jews lived next to the maharajah's palace. Therefore, who better to act as mediator between the ambitious trading powers and the royal family of Cochin?

The significance of Joseph Rabban in the history of Jewish-Indo relations meant that both the older Malabari Jews and the Paradesis needed to claim him as their own. Although the Whites and Blacks had initially integrated on some level, this was to change. In their studies, Katz and Goldberg note that the community split along colour lines, reflecting the indigenous caste system of the Kerala Hindus. Although such caste divisions were a breach of Jewish law, or *Halakha*, the practice became entrenched.

Anthropologist David Mandelbaum believes the distinction was introduced by the Jews from Europe and the Middle East, including those who fled religious persecution in Spain and Portugal in the sixteenth century. The new arrivals boasted of their Jewish lineage and greater Jewish knowledge compared with the Malabari Jews, who had been isolated from the rest of the world and therefore lacked the sophistication of the European Jews.

There were two main sub-castes in the Cochini Jewry. Those who claimed their families originated in Israel were deemed to be superior. The other key sign of superiority was a lineage going back to Cranganore – those Jews who traced their ancestry back to Rabban were seen to have come from a line of kings and therefore had a higher status in Indian society.

Cochini Jewish scholars note that the Paradesi Jews linked skin colour to religious purity. They claimed their pale skin made them the only pure Jews of Kerala, and they also laid claim to links with Cranganore. In the Paradesis' version of history, the Malabari Jews, far from being the inheritors of the King of Shingly, were the offspring of slave converts.

Mandelbaum, one of the most respected authorities on the subject, speculated that the Cranganore Jews must have had some mixed blood. The Jewish merchants and crew who came to Malabar at the time of Solomon were unlikely to have made the dangerous journey with their wives and children. They will have married and lived with local women, who gave birth to their children, who became Jews. If this

was so, how could the Paradesis claim Jewish purity as well as Cranganore ancestry?

Much of the history was oral and there were no documents to prove that the White Jews had never intermarried with the locals when they first arrived. Yet this claim of purity, of pure Jewish ancestry, led the Paradesis to claim a natural ascendancy.

In caste-based India, where the concept of religious purity is paramount, the taint of slavery eventually undermined the Malabaris' standing in the royal court of Cochin. Loss of status and economic influence was only part of the cost they had to bear. Dubbed the sons of slaves, the Black Jews were then barred from marrying the White Jews, barred from the Paradesi Synagogue, barred from forming their own place of worship in their homes.

It is true that such colour-based divisions existed even among other Jewish communities in India, such as the Bene Israel community in Bombay. But in Cochin it was highly institutionalized. Rabbis of the fifteenth and sixteenth century were aware of the issue and ruled it was wrong to discriminate against the Black Jews. In 1520 Rabbi David ben Solomon ibn Zimra wrote a letter in Hebrew from Cairo to the Cochini community, in which he noted there was a smaller group known as the *meyuchasim*, or Jews 'with a pedigree', who refused to mix with the other Jewish community, whom they referred to as 'slaves'. The Cochini Jews were told that inter-marriage between the two communities was allowed after performing a prayer ritual of conversion – that would eliminate

any doubts the White Jews had about the purity of the Black community. Such a ritual would mean it was wrong to refer to the Black Jews as slaves. But the rabbi's advice was ignored by the Paradesis.

The question that remains is why did the Jews create a divide among themselves when they had come to India to escape persecution in Europe? The answer was money and power: the Black Jews had it; the White Jews wanted it. Forty years after the petition to Rabbi ibn Zimra, the Paradesis' economic and social status rose as the other group's declined. The Paradesis had secured land from the king next to his palace to build a synagogue. They were in close proximity and in an ideal position to press their case. In the end, the Brahmin maharajah favoured the fair-skinned and 'pure' minority.

In Solomon's time, the link between justice and shalom was inviolable. Without justice there could be no harmony, no fertility, no shalom. Cochin's division, which became known as the 'Jewish apartheid', went against this tenet of faith. Kerala's Jewry turned on one another. And it would take centuries of campaigning by the Black Jews and eventually a black civil-rights leader known as the 'Jewish Gandhi' to deliver justice in Cochin.

Six

Opium Traders and Oil Pressers:
The Lost Tribes

'And it shall come to pass in that day
That the Lord will set his hand again the second time
To recover the remnant of His people...'

Isaiah, 11:11

The Jews of Kerala are acknowledged as the oldest in India, yet there are others with an equally rich heritage: the Bene Israel community, or 'Sons of Israel', who are based in Bombay, and the Baghdadi Jews, who have now all but disappeared. All three communities have been the subject of much speculation as to whether they originated from Israel's Ten Lost Tribes, who vanished almost three millennia ago. What happened to these tribes remains one of the mysteries of Judaism.

Before his death, Moses bequeathed command of the twelve tribes of his people to Joshua, who went on to conquer

the land of Canaan around 1200 BCE, according to the Bible. The land was eventually divided between these tribes. Judah and Benjamin took the southern territories, which would become the Kingdom of Judah, while the remaining ten tribes took the land which would become the Kingdom of Israel. In 722 BCE Israel fell to the Assyrians and its people were dispersed. The Bible maintains that the Jews safeguarded their religious identity in foreign lands and prophesies that one day they would be reunited in the Holy Land. The story of the Lost Tribes remains an inviolable belief for many Jews. It ensnared the imagination of chroniclers, with accounts of communities that survived despite their displacement in alien lands. It has been suggested that the Jews of India are among the Lost Tribes, alongside the Falashas of Ethiopia and Pathans of Afghanistan.

*

Today the Bene Israel Jews are the largest of the community in India, with a fairly stable population of around 5,000 people. Tradition says they arrived in India some time between the eighth and sixth century BCE. They were travelling along the western Konkan coast when their boat was shipwrecked during a storm near Navagaon, which lies some 48 kilometres south of modern-day Mumbai. The community claims only seven women and seven men survived the tragedy, with the rest perishing in the treacherous Arabian Sea. The few bodies that were recovered were buried in a cemetery at Navagaon.

The seven original couples grew into a community of thousands and lived in rural Maharashtra.

There are different theories as to their origins. One was that they hailed from the Holy Land in the time of Elijah, which explains why that prophet has a central place in their traditions. Another theory was they were Persian or Yemeni. Either way, the Jews found themselves in an alien landscape, hemmed in by streams and mountains. They faced the apocalyptic sight of their first Indian monsoon, when the sky turned black, coastal winds bent the palm trees into submission and ceaseless rains engulfed all around, turning soil into slurry and causing roiling rivers to overwhelm their banks. Yet they acclimatized and settled. They eventually took up oil pressing, adapting their traditional skill of using olives. They established farms, cultivated coconut groves and sold their produce. Others took up skilled work such as carpentry. The community would work for six days and on the Sabbath they rested. One account from 1917, *A Short Account of the Calcutta Jews, with a Sketch of the Bene-Israels, the Cochin Jews, the Chinese Jews and the Black Jews of Abyssinia* by I. A. Isaac, described their plight thus:

> Homeless, penniless, ignorant of the language of the country and unaccustomed to the scorching Indian sun, they took to agriculture and oil pressing. Their abstinence from work on Saturdays earned them the sobriquet of 'Sabbath oil pressers'.

In *The Jews of India*, published by the Israel Museum in

Jerusalem, their religious rituals are described as being 'based on biblical Judaism: they celebrated Jewish holidays related to the Bible; the Sabbath was strictly observed; all male children were circumcised eight days after birth'. Their guidance was provided by religious leaders called *kazis*, who ruled on Jewish matters and were often seen by local authorities as leaders who could deal with disputes. Initially the community had no synagogue or Torah scrolls, replying purely upon their spiritual leaders.

By the seventeenth century, the British East India Company had established itself in Bombay, now called Mumbai. Bombay grew into the most important trading port in India and employment boomed, attracting thousands of people from across the sub-continent. One imagines that the mood of expansion and boundless opportunity may be similar to the economic renaissance that India is witnessing right now, as millions migrate from the villages to the cities looking for a stake in the capitalist revolution. The Bene Israel people also migrated from the countryside to the big city, drawn by the promise of an easier living. The community thrived. Many worked for the East India Company, while others enlisted in the military, where several achieved high rank and were awarded decorations for bravery. Others worked in construction or the bustling shipyards which furnished the trading boom of the British Empire with ships for Indian goods. The oil-pressing tradition died out, eventually, as other players had already captured that particular market.

Their first synagogue, Sha'ar haRahamim, was founded

in the city in 1796 by Commandant Samuel Ezekiel Divekar. He was something of a hero, being one of the few soldiers to survive capture by the forces of the Sultan of Mysore and being held as a prisoner of war. During his captivity he made a promise: if he survived imprisonment, he would build a synagogue for the Bene Israel of Bombay. He had heard of them from his contact with the Jews of Cochin. The war hero was as good as his word.

The synagogue proved to be just the beginning and by 1838, the community had grown to 8,000 – more than the Cochini and Baghdadi Jews put together. Eventually in 1875 a Hebrew-Marathi School was established in Bombay, known as the Israelite School. As educational establishments such as these flourished, the level of literacy rose among the community and a number graduated as advocates, physicians, engineers, accountants and civil servants. On the whole the community was not entrepreneurial and preferred safe jobs, often in government services.

Relations in India's cosmopolitan melting pot were good. Each community respected the religious practices of the other. As the Jewish community became established it started to use nearby Pune as a summer retreat. Some Jews took jobs which involved them being stationed throughout the Indian empire, so the community branched out to new cities, including Ahmedabad, Delhi and Karachi in modern-day Pakistan. These satellite communities never comprised more than a handful of Jews, so they were not troubled by the ruling Mughal powers of the north, where the dominant

Hindus and Sikhs faced merciless persecution at times during this era.

While British rule lasted, the educated Bene Israel did well. By the 1940s the community had reached a peak of 25,000 people in India. The Bene Israel were like the Cochinis in that they, too, differentiated between light- and dark-skinned Jews, mirroring the indigenous society, which also put a premium on fairness. The difference is that the Bene Israel to this day number thousands – evidence of their ability to overcome their divisions in time and survive.

Like the Cochinis, they too caught the attention of visiting foreigners, who recognized them as a distinct people from the Indians. One European Jewish traveller, Henry Shoskes, records his encounter in 1947 in *Your World and Mine*. He was clearly moved to find these lost Jews in the heart of India:

> Their garb and their complexion seemed foreign, but their eyes shining like little stars were as unmistakably Jewish as those of our boys in Poland who used to chant the Friday evening prayers with similar enthusiasm... Choking with emotion, Cynowicz and I joined in the song. We did not mind the strangeness of the tune, the words or their meaning; the faith they expressed was the same as we have always known.

But the axis of events in 1947 and 1948 – Indian Independence and the creation of Israel – would usher in irrevocable change. The Bene Israel became concerned for their economic

prospects under the new political order in India as many had depended on the British Raj for their survival. The combined lure of Zionism and new opportunities in Israel led many to leave for ever.

*

The Raj was pivotal to the fortunes of all the Jews of India. The rise of Bombay under the British led to Cochin's eventual demise as the premier trading port of the west coast, which in turn impacted on the fortunes of the Jews there. In Bombay itself, the transformation that took place as a result of British trade led the Bene Israel people to migrate from village to city and to tie their fortunes with the Raj. In the case of the Baghdadi Jews of Bombay and Calcutta, they came to India around 1760 from the Persian Gulf port of Basra, which was another outpost of the British Empire. Jews involved in trade with India arrived from Basra and Baghdad, at first settling on the western coast of India. A community of one hundred Jews formed an Arabic-speaking Jewish colony in Surat. These merchants were named Baghdadi or Iraqi Jews, and in time others from Syria, Persia and Afghanistan joined them. As Surat declined, important Jewish families such as the Sassoons, Abrahams, Ezras and Kadouries moved towards the new British-ruled commercial hubs of Bombay and Calcutta. Fortunes were made through trade in cotton, jute, tobacco and opium.

Within a century of their move to India, the Arabic-

speaking Jewish community numbered almost thirty families. The centre of their religious life was a house rented from Parsis, who hailed originally from Persia. Thus the old world and the new conspired to survive.

The most famous of the Baghdadi Jews, whose name resonates in India to this day, is David Sassoon, who arrived in Bombay in 1833. His family had held the post of chief treasurer to the governor of Baghdad, and he forged his own legacy in India as the head of a trading dynasty which would eventually stretch from Calcutta and Bombay to Shanghai and Singapore. He became a renowned philanthropist, which together with his commercial pedigree earned him the appellation of 'the Rothschild of the East'.

Among his charitable activities was the building of the Magen David synagogue in Bombay in 1861, which included a religious school and hostel. Jews from across India found jobs in the Sassoon factories in Bombay. His corporate ethos was based on patrician values: he took it upon himself to provide food and accommodation for Jews arriving in the city, as well as arranging medical care and schooling for the children. The schools even taught ritual slaughter to ensure that families who were posted to remote areas far from other Jews could maintain their religious practices.

Sassoon's contribution to Bombay life was acknowledged beyond his own people. On his death in 1864, the *Times of India* wrote that 'Bombay has lost one of its most energetic, wealthy, public spirited and benevolent citizens...' His successors continued his work of building a textile empire

and also endowed charities and schools, and built cemeteries for the Baghdadi Jews of Bombay.

The second largest group of Baghdadi Jews settled in Calcutta, which was India's eastern trading port. Many were Iraqis who had fled the tyranny of the Daud Pasha (1817–31). The founding father of this branch of the Baghdadi Jews was Moses Dwek ha Cohen, who acted as head of the community, honorary rabbi and *mohel*, according to *The Jews of India*. They earned their living by becoming merchants in the lucrative trade of opium, silk, indigo and jute, and by the nineteenth century had grown to some 1,800 people. A few worked in finance or became landowners. The Ezra and Elias families were dominant players here, like Sassoon, leading the way in creating employment as well as charitable activities.

I. A. Isaac describes how the Ezras were the drug barons of their day, exporting opium from Calcutta to South-East Asia. David Joseph Ezra exported opium to Hong Kong, as well as dealing in more innocuous cargo. He acted as the agent for Arabian ships arriving in Calcutta to offload dates and other produce from Muscat and Zanzibar. Opium was just one of many revenue earners in his commercial portfolio.

While the Baghdadi Jews were unsentimental in business, they were diligent in matters of religion. These same families helped build a series of synagogues, starting with Calcutta's Neveh Shalom in 1831. In both cities the Baghdadi Jews maintained their Iraqi Jewish traditions, as well as Arabic as their first language. They were well regarded by the British rulers and many were named honorary magistrates.

One unfortunate side effect of this closeness to the British was a negative attitude among the Baghdadis towards the indigenous Indians. 'The Baghdadis wished to assimilate into British society and be considered European,' according to *The Jews of India*. As a result they aped European dress and lifestyle, as well as prejudices. The wealthier ones spoke English, not Hindi, Bengali and Marathi, the local Indian languages. They sought to join the stuffy and elitist English clubs – a bizarre little world of afternoon tea and dainty sandwiches, with cricket on the lawns followed by cocktails on the terrace: an Anglicized haven where the Brits could convene in private, away from the 'natives'.

The Baghdadis' taste for social stratification extended to their fellow Jews. While Cochin's White or Paradesi Jews were warmly accepted by them, the darker skinned Malabari and Bene Israel Jews were not. This mirrored the attitudes of the Paradesis in Cochin who also sought to play up their fairness, Jewish purity and European savoir-faire in order to court the approval of the ruling elite.

For the Baghdadis, affiliation to the Raj spelled doom when the sun finally set on the British Empire in India. After Indian Independence in 1947, the Baghdadi Jews found their position uncertain. The socialist-inspired government of the new India ushered in import and foreign exchange controls which hit the Jews' business hard. The formation of Israel in 1948 also gave birth to an era of Arab-Israeli tensions in the Middle East which further impeded the trading opportunities of the Baghdadis. For example, the key markets of

Iraq and Egypt were both closed to their trading activities.

In the 1940s, the once-invincible Sassoon family closed its factory gates, making thousands of Jews unemployed. By 1973 the mills of the Elias family in Calcutta had also shut down. The result was economic misery, followed by exodus, with many Jews going to Israel or to the West to start a new life. By the mid-1990s, a community that was 5,000 strong in its heyday had collapsed to less than 200, a decline as precipitous as the Cochinis. Unlike them, the Baghdadis never preserved their identity once they moved overseas. It seems the Baghdadis really are, in this sense at least, a lost tribe.

Seven

Son of Salem

*'Courage has never been known to be a matter of muscle;
it is a matter of the heart. The toughest muscle has been
known to tremble before an imaginary fear. It was the
heart that set the muscle trembling.'*

Gandhi, *Book of Quotations*, 1931

Every town has its maverick. In Mattancheri's Jew Town that
man was Gamy Salem: self-confessed cynic, scourge of con-
vention and one who viewed the Cochini Jews' chequered
history with an unsparingly critical eye. He came from one of
the Cochini Jews' most distinguished dynasties, a family of
iconoclasts. His father had been known as the 'Jewish
Gandhi'.

The elder Salem had five children: two daughters and three
sons. The sons, Raymond, Balfour and Gamy, all inherited the
Salem spirit, but only Gamy survives. In the 1950s Gamy's
brother Balfour defied the conservative White elders by marrying Baby Koder, daughter of a prominent White Jewish family.

It was the first intermarriage between Black and White Jews and blew away the old dividing line. In a way, Balfour was continuing his father's work of breaking down barriers. Where A. B. Salem had used the law and non-violent protests like his mentor, Gandhi, his son Balfour changed local history by standing by his love for Baby.

Gamy also followed his brother in marrying a White Jewess, Reema, although things were much easier by the time their turn came. Sitting in his front parlour on Synagogue Lane, we would talk for hours on end. I came to enjoy our afternoon interludes over glasses of fizzy Mirinda and snacks. 'Jew Town's sole sceptic', as he called himself, was a welcome relief from the prickliness of some of his neighbours. His approach to life was not bound by the strictures of orthodoxy and status. One sensed that for Gamy, the world held deeper pleasures, more sparkling sensations than those of the synagogue and tradition. Here was an old man with a taste for trouble and an appetite for wider possibilities in life, even now, in his eighth decade.

When it came to his community, he feigned indifference, even amusement at this narrow little world, yet clearly he was deeply bound to it – despite his best efforts to disguise the fact that he cared. He remained one of the few willing to confront the past and future honestly. As one of the Black Jews in Ernakulam put it, 'Gamy's the only fellow over there who's not a damned fool.'

Although, sometimes he liked to play the fool. He was both funny and kind. Strangers were drawn to his door by the

tantalizing delights of easy conversation, bad jokes, worse whisky and fizzy drinks that glowed like radioactive waste. Seeing me stalking Synagogue Lane, day in, day out, amused him. He would watch me from his doorway, feign horror, pretend to hide and then tease me about Sammy Hallegua: 'Your Enemy Number One has gone to the market. I can talk for two minutes, then I have an urgent appointment to play bridge with my old ladies in Fort Cochin.' He wasn't kidding about timing conversations. If he said he'd give you two minutes and spent fifteen with you, next time you came by, he'd tell you that you were already in debt with him and he would not extend any more credit. I couldn't help liking him and his wife.

A handsome man with the darker complexion common among Keralites, he had a head of steel grey hair and sported the local dress of short-sleeved shirt hanging loose over a white cotton checked lungi tied at the waist. Reema was still a great beauty, with a flawless milky complexion, smooth forehead and the clear bright eyes of woman years younger. Together, they were a striking couple. So opposite in looks and temperament, yet, like all really happy couples, when together they were seamless. They seemed to be relatively untouched by the melancholy that permeated the neighbour-hood, although there were times when they too succumbed.

Their home was simple, with a long corridor-style living room that opened straight on to the street through shuttered doors. Through to the right was a dining room, with table and chairs, a fridge and walls adorned with huge framed

family photos, including one of A. B. Salem. Black-and-white stills of the Jews in their heyday, dressed up and partying, as well as shiny, bright snaps of grandchildren. Their Christian servant, Mary, a diminutive old lady only four feet ten inches tall and dressed in a floral kaftan, would flit in and out of the living room as she went about her chores. She had just had her cataracts removed, paid for by her master. Rather incongruously, she wore glamorous Jackie Onassis-style dark glasses that engulfed her tiny features as she polished and tidied and went about her work. Now and then she would come over and stand listening to us, her head on one side, even though her English was minimal. Her ease reflected that of her employers, for this was a happy house. And the master was never happier than when playing mischief. It was his chief pastime on a street where little happened any more. He had a keen eye for comedy and would gather scurrilous scraps of gossip and feed these titbits to his wife and friends. Nothing was sacred or exempt from his humour, not even the synagogue. Pomposity, greed and vanity were favourite targets.

One afternoon, as I took my habitual rest in his front room, a couple of visitors going to Sarah's house caught Gamy's attention. The unwitting prey for his caustic wit was a father and his sixteen-year-old son. They were converted Christians from Chennai, from across the state line in Tamil Nadu. Gamy began to tell me their story, his right hand occasionally lifting to his mouth as if to suppress a guffaw.

'See these two here. I call them Fool Number One and

Fool Number Two. They're low-caste Hindus who converted
to Christianity. Why? They were poor people and they thought
it would bring a better life. Only thing, nobody got rich from
going to church. They hear about the White Jews. Old people,
big houses and no children. Understand?'

I looked at this poor couple, wreathed in sweat as they
struggled down the street with numerous heavy bags of food
shopping, and felt an instinctive dread about their story.

'They come to Jew Town, they meet Sarah. They become
friends. Our Sarah's no fool, unlike our visitors from Chennai.'
He sniggers, then sucks his teeth back in. 'She tells them she
cannot get quality vegetables in Cochin market, that the food
is better in Chennai. So, every two weeks our friends come by
train across the mountains, carrying heavy bags of Sarah's
favourite fruit and vegetables. From Chennai. For free!'

'Are these foods only available in Chennai?'

'Same food as from here! These are poor people, they
cannot afford. Yet they bring free food. And Sarah lets them
do it.'

'If they can't afford it, why do it?'

'They believe when Sarah dies, they'll inherit her house.
Everyone knows about Jew Town. So, the vultures fly across
the mountains of Kerala, fly in from the villages and towns, to
come and wait for their chance. The young Muslim boys who
sell postcards outside her house. You know them?'

'Yes.'

'Same story.' He wobbled his head in affirmation.

'Has she promised the Chennai people the house?'

'Sarah's already made provisions for her will. These fellows won't get it. Her young Muslim boys won't get it. But Sarah's smart. While she lives, everyone is dancing to her tune.'

The real estate on Synagogue Lane was expensive. This was one of the most important tourist destinations in Kerala, attracting caravans of visitors every day from across India. But more importantly, it was a place that drew rich foreigners, not just of Jewish origin, but of every background. For that reason, everyone wanted a piece of Jew Town. It was a point that was not lost on any of the Paradesis. This was also part of their defensiveness: the fear that people were waiting, quite literally, to slide into their slippers.

Gamy told me the Chennai family was so keen to win Sarah's favour that they were planning to convert once again – this time to Judaism. On the last visit, the father had informed Gamy he planned to have his teenage son circumcised. I was about to hear the story for myself, as the Chennai couple popped in to see old uncle Gamy. The father, a small and immaculately turned out man in his forties, gingerly hovered on the threshold. His tall, shy son stood awkwardly behind him with a look of suffering on his face that seemed out of place.

Gamy nodded towards the doorway, then turned to me and said, *sotto voce*: 'Here he comes, Circumcision Boy.'

'Uncleji. I've brought my son to see you. We've just seen Aunty and she is well.'

'Come, come,' said Gamy, the generous host. He introduced

them and offered them a seat on the sofa, but they insisted on standing, in an uncomfortable, deferential mode in front of Gamy's planter's chair. They may have left Hinduism behind for Christianity and now Judaism, but the old caste mentality was harder to relinquish.

'Uncleji,' the father began hesitantly, eyes lowered and palms in namaste, 'we have some good news.' He gently pushed his son forward towards Gamy.

'My boy has had the great honour of being circumcised,' he announced proudly.

Gamy paused at this momentous pronouncement, took in a sharp breath and then turned to the boy, clasping his hands in congratulations.

'Ah, but this is terrific news. And, tell me, where did they do it?'

There was a long pause.

'Chennai,' said the boy in a strangled voice. 'Two days ago.'

I offered my congratulations to him as he blushed terribly. It was traumatic enough to be circumcised at sixteen, without being dragged across two states to deliver vegetables to a wily old lady in Cochin and then have his most intimate news conveyed to the whole town. All this and he was still technically a Christian.

'Did it hurt, Baba?'

'Uncleji, it was very painful,' the boy confirmed, head wobbling in agitation as he twisted his legs from one side to the other, either in embarrassment or pain, or both.

'You've done a great thing,' said Gamy. 'Many congratulations.'

With that, the father and son clasped Gamy's hands once
more and gazed into his eyes with gratitude, murmuring
thanks. Their action had met with approval. The boy then
touched the old man's feet in the traditional act of deference
and they announced they were on their way home, all the way
back to Tamil Nadu. As they headed off towards the bus stop,
Gamy turned to me and said archly, 'Now you are knowing
why I'm calling them Fools Number One and Two.'

*

Synagogue Lane was in the midst of the festivals. It had
commemorated the Day of Atonement, a day for reflection,
remorse and prayer for renewal. It had celebrated Sukkoth,
the feast of the Tabernacles, which remembered the ancient
Jews' time in the desert.

Now they were preparing for two of the most joyous
celebrations: Shmini and Simhat Torah. It had taken a whole
week to prepare the synagogue and the feasts that would
accompany the occasion. Today, although Sammy and the
community still carefully observed all the proper preparations
and customs, there was none of the thrilling anticipation that
marked the old days.

As I sat in a café just moments from their street I pondered
their old life. Images of the festivals of previous generations,
with the men dressed in their best suits, the ladies in their

finest embroidered saris, jewels twinkling at their white throats and ears; impish children, blushes of pink in fat cheeks, black curls dancing at their temples as they tore up and down Synagogue Lane, sticky pockets crammed with festival sweets.

The festival was nothing without the food. I would taste a real Cochini Jewish banquet in my time here and it was some of the best food I have ever had. I remember an Indian friend telling me once, 'Food reflects its people. Bland food makes for bland human beings.'

The Cochini Jews' food was a fusion not just of Israel and India, but of the rest of the world. These people had come from Israel, across the Middle East, from Portugal, Spain, Germany and other places over the centuries. When one tasted the dishes of the Cochini Jews, it was a sensory reminder that this was a migratory people who had been banished, found asylum in disparate lands and absorbed the best they had to offer. Their food bore the traces of all these adoptive cultures, while remaining very much Jewish in terms of which foods were eaten, how it was prepared and, of course, the symbolism that accompanied the simplest acts such as the breaking of bread. Wherever they travelled to, wherever they found sanctuary, the Jews carried their history in their recipes, each dish an evocation of exile, a tribute to their homeland.

I drank down my milkshake, paid the bill and came knocking at Gamy's door, part of my daily ritual. He greeted me warmly and then, after scanning the Hallegua house to check the warden was not around, he invited me in. Reema

was out and Gamy was in the middle of an important business transaction. The fish wallah had just arrived on his bicycle with the day's catch. The two were locked in negotiations over the contents of the wicker basket which was covered with a wet muslin cloth to keep the fish fresh. Gamy lifted the cloth, peered and prodded at the bounty within. Ali, the Muslim fishmonger, talked through the catch as though discussing the merits of uncut diamonds. Once the choice was made, he took the fish through to Gamy's kitchen at the back and collected payment.

He warmly wished Gamy goodbye and then mounted his bike again, his plaintive cry telling the neighbourhood that the fish was in. Gamy went to re-examine his purchase, evidently delighted. For a South Indian, there are few sights more uplifting than a fat, wet fish. I asked him if the fish was for the festival, but he said this was nothing special, unlike the sea bass that Babu had purchased. Word had spread to Mattancheri of the Ernakulam Jews' good fortune. I sensed a tinge of envy as Gamy commented, 'I hear he paid over 1,000 rupees. I doubt it will be worth the price.'

The thought of glistening sea bass at festival time summoned up the memory of tables laden for past celebrations. 'We used to have such a pukka Jewish life,' Gamy sighed. 'We used to celebrate like hell!'

Yet when the others left for Israel, Gamy and Reema stayed.

'Israel is in our prayers. Of course it is. It's something like our religious duty. But I'm very happy I didn't go to live there.

I've been there four or five times. Not bad! But we have a better life here. Why lose that?'

He gestured to the street in explanation, to the palms, to the sea, to the ease of having a fishmonger come to your door, with whom you could exchange pleasantries and allow into your kitchen to wash your fish and cool it in a dish of water. Small things like this made it hard to leave. But he was in a minority. Not even his own children felt this way about India and all the good things it had given the Jews: land, security, peace. His children had gone in search of jobs and partners overseas.

'There weren't any prospects for marriage here, then, to allow them to stay?'

'Have you met any young people here? Have you even seen any?' he said, his face a mask of incredulity. 'You know who they are. Yaheh is here. Keith is here. Stay or go. He doesn't know what to do. He wanted to get married, long ago. Yaheh's sister he would have married. When he couldn't have her, he didn't want the other. End of story.'

'I told you, everybody is waiting for the end now.' He sighed as he rose from his favourite spot to fetch some more water. He returned bearing two glasses of iced panni. He sipped from his glass, eyes closing as he winced at the coldness of the water. 'If I die tomorrow, these people – ' he pointed to the postcard hawkers who were now eavesdropping outside his doorway – 'Muslims will have to carry me to my grave. Because there are not enough of our own men. Our dead, they never used to be touched by outsiders. Now there's no option.'

Outside it turned dark as the clouds heralded another storm. Gamy went to turn on the single low-wattage light bulb in the living room, but the electricity had cut out, which was typical enough. He slumped back into his chair as if exhausted by the effort, chin dipped towards his chest, and resumed where he had left off. He had a theory as to why things had panned out this way, he told me. The Jews had once been lucky, he said. 'They caught the right people.' In the same way a wise fisherman knew where he could most profitably cast his net. 'We caught people who could help us, like the raja. We were canny that way.' The Cochini Jewry were given the most perfect set of circumstances and yet still things got spoiled.

The history of prejudice against the Blacks by the Whites had jinxed them, Gamy said. It was the old Jewish belief in the link between justice and shalom. 'There is some curse in this town,' he said softly, with all the melodrama that only a Jewish Indian can muster. His eyes shone, long yellow teeth protruding slightly as he warmed to his theme. 'Nobody will ever rise above average. It's true!' he insisted, now sitting forward in his chair.

'So many of us were smart. Brilliant, even. Brilliant minds from rich families, high connections, a great history. But where has it got us? To the edge of extinction. Is it our curse? We had eight synagogues, the Blacks and Whites, a history that went back to the great age of Solomon. Now there's one synagogue here, two are empty in Ernakulam. And the rest? Vanished or crumbling into ruins, homes to snakes

and rats. We're just fifty where there were once thousands.'

He went quiet again, jutting his jaw out as he scratched the bristly grey stubble on his chin. Clearly, for all the jokes, it troubled him deeply. Gamy saw that a collective malaise had descended on the White Jews in particular. It was a recurring theme in the faded salons of Synagogue Lane: talk of curse, of retribution, each yet another incarnation of the intolerable guilt that pressed down upon their necks like cold stone. Most of the White Jews were old. Those who were not old were depressed, sick, reclusive or unmarried. The rest were buried in the graveyard just a few hundred yards away, a walled cemetery with the gate bolted and padlocked to keep out tourists and drunks, who came there at night to lie on the gravestones and drink toddy. After several nocturnal episodes of drunken carousing and reports of urination on the tombstones, the Jews decided to keep the cemetery permanently locked. It had come to this: even their final resting place was the subject of irreverence and defilement.

Gamy rubbed his hand across his face; his eyes were weary and as bloodshot as those of Yaheh's hound. He needed to rest, but he staved off sleep's entreaties. His promise of talking for only five minutes was forsaken as he wanted to talk and talk, as if expressing the thoughts that had corrupted his mind over time would expel them finally.

'You know, you mustn't blame Sammy for not speaking of this,' he said gently.

'I don't. I can see why he's like this.'

'He's not a bad man. He's a good man who carries a

burden. Our history, the source of our curse. Look at the fate of Jew Town. Are we not being punished by God?' He looked at me intently, the expression on his face giving the answer. 'Young people have had to leave to escape its curse. All the children have gone. If they stay, what do they have? No scope here, no future, no marriage partners. What's this, if not a curse?'

'Why a curse still? Your own father ended the divide. It's over.'

'Yes. My father did his best to stop it. But he was too late to save us.'

His father was a subject he rarely discussed, even with the other Cochinis. In the past, he had resisted having this conversation but now he relented. I was to discover it was not easy being the son of Salem. It was an awesome legacy, one which should have inspired pride in all Jews, Black and White. While other Indians fought the great political battle of the time, for independence from the British, Salem also fought for freedom. But his battle was at home, in his own street, at his synagogue.

Abraham Barak Salem was born into a poor family in 1882 but rose from his modest background to become the first graduate among his people. Armed with his degree in law, he shunned the chance to become a politician of national stature to focus on local issues instead. He was a natural populist, fighting the cause of the ordinary man, the underdog. He would make his public addresses from a hillside in Ernakulum which was dubbed 'Salem Hill' in tribute to this

fiery orator. It became a kind of Speaker's Corner, devoted to the passionate monologues of just one man, who would give vent to his anger, advocating his case to the treetops, issuing his demand for justice to the clouds.

In the end people heeded him. In Jew Town today, one of the approach roads to the synagogue is called A. B. Salem Road, the same synagogue that he was once barred from entering.

After the creation of Israel, A. B. Salem was also tasked with going to the new motherland to plead the case of Malabari Jews wishing to emigrate there. At first there were some obstacles to their migration because of incidents of elephantiasis among the Cochin Jews. Elephantiasis is an insect-borne disease which causes the head or limbs to swell to huge proportions. A. B. Salem went to Israel to explain that this was not a condition that could be spread and therefore was no danger to the fledgling nation. After his special plead-ing, the Israeli authorities relented and the ban was relaxed. Ironically, his success marked the beginning of the end for the community and the way of life that he strived so hard to safeguard.

But his greatest success was fighting for the religious equality of the Black Jews. Taking his cue from Gandhi's non-violent form of protest in the fight for Indian Independence, Salem applied similar tactics among the Paradesi community. By the late 1940s he had succeeded in winning certain rights for his people. Gandhi's methods would eventually spread beyond India, inspiring Martin Luther King during the

American civil-rights movement as well as shaping Nelson Mandela's own political philosophy in South Africa to bridge the divide between Black and White. In Jew Town, the achievements of its own local hero were not universally acknowledged. Recognition of Salem's legacy was inevitably an admission of guilt for some of the Whites.

Even in Salem's old house, one sensed his own son had conflicting feelings when discussing those days. For Gamy it awakened emotions I had never expected: reticence, but, more surprisingly, disappointment and even bitterness. His father was a great man. But Gamy felt he could have been greater had he lifted his eyes beyond the small-town feud of the Cochini Jews to the bigger picture of the Indian Independence movement that swept across India. As a talented young Jewish lawyer, Salem attracted the attention of India's most glittering political son, Jawaharlal Nehru. He was invited by Nehru to participate in a key National Congress meeting. It could have been the political break of a lifetime, catapulting him into national consciousness, but in the end Salem chose the synagogue.

'He should have been a great man, but he ended up being a very small man. You know, he had the potential to be a senior leader at national level, given his intellect and contacts. To know Nehru and Gandhi personally, to be a distinguished lawyer, to be one of the brightest of his generation.'

It had not been an easy journey, coming from the poor community of the Ernakulam Black Jews. To attend the Madras law college, he had to take a boat, a bullock cart and

then the train to Madras. He was the first in his community to graduate and once his youngest son, Gamy, was born, he moved the family to Mattancheri, where they remained.

Gamy felt his father wasted his talents on Jew Town, which did not deserve him. Yet without A. B. Salem, equality would have taken longer. Salem fought and won important causes for his people, he raised children who went on to become doctors, engineers, lawyers. He earned the respect of most of the community. What was this, if not greatness? Yet Gamy was unconvinced. Equality came to Cochin, but it arrived too late. His father had squandered talent and ambition on a cause that was doomed to failure.

'If he had stuck to politics, he could have been a great man, but he preferred the synagogue, the Jewish community, the festivals. He was obsessed with local issues. He had a mirror, "Salem's Looking Glass" we called it, where he pasted newspaper clippings, ideas, issues that caught his interest. He would take these issues and fight for them, go to his hillside and speak for hours to ordinary people who came and listened. His aim in life was to bring up the poor people, but at the same time he brought himself down.'

In India, politics is the route to pursuing not just lofty purposes, but also personal enrichment and aggrandizement. In an arena awash with dirty ambition, Salem had remained true to the values of his faith, to the importance of justice in the community.

I felt Gamy was being tough on his father but, as he himself recognized, perhaps this was because he felt he had

also failed to live up to his potential. Gamy had always dreamed of getting out, escaping, shaking off Jew Town's strictures to explore a world that sang to his adventurous soul. He had the chance and he blew it. He could not forgive himself. Nor could he forgive his father, whose chances had been even greater.

'I find fault with my father, I find fault with myself,' he told me, in confessional mood that stormy afternoon just before the onset of Shabbat. 'I went to the US, studied with a scholarship at Cornell, but came back here, got stuck, ended in same position. Same thing. Same fate. So who am I to criticize? But I did not have my father's talent. I'm just an average person compared to him.'

'Aren't you proud of your father's efforts?'

'Of course I'm proud. But I would've been prouder if he'd answered the calls to greater things that kept knocking at his door. He ignored those calls.'

Despite choosing this path and resisting the lure of national politics, Salem maintained close relations with the Nehru dynasty, which brought the Kerala Jews to prominence, once again enabling the community to punch above its weight for a little while longer. One such example was when Nehru accompanied his daughter Indira Gandhi to visit the synagogue. The synagogue was even immortalized on an Indian stamp one year. Jew Town was a valuable symbol of India's secular ideal, demonstrating its long tradition of religious tolerance.

Down the timeline of Cochini Jewish history, there are

moments that resonate through the millennia: the first contact with the kingdom of Solomon; the fall of the Second Temple; the arrival of Joseph Rabban on Indian shores; the loss of Cranganore and the arrival of the Jews from Europe who would initiate divide between Black and White. In the late nineteenth century, the powerful advocacy of a Black Jew would restore Judaism's ancient tradition of imparting justice. Salem built upon the work of those before him, faceless heroes, as well as his own grandfather, who fought for centuries to break the colour bar of Jew Town. This was Cochin's civil-rights movement. It started in the sixteenth century and did not end until America's own campaign for equality was at its height in the 1950s and 1960s. The fight began where it ended: in the Paradesi Synagogue, the focal point in the quest for equality.

Eight

Segregation in the Synagogue

'You must not be guilty of unjust verdicts...
You must not slander your own people...
You must not bear hatred for your brother in your own
  heart...
If a stranger lives with you in your land, do not molest
  him...
You must count him as one of your countrymen and love
  him as yourself – for you yourselves were once
  strangers in Egypt.'

Leviticus, 19:1–2, 11–18

After the loss of the Second Temple, the Jewish people were bereft. They believed they had been abandoned by God. The Temple had represented the divine presence amongst them and as such it was the focal point of their faith. Its destruction for a second time led the Jews to believe that it was wrong to cherish ambitions to resurrect the Temple a third time: it was

not Yahweh's wish. Instead they would find a new way to worship, and in the end they substituted the synagogue for the Temple in their day-to-day prayers.

Shabbat was celebrated here, providing a new setting for the Jews to commune directly with the divine. The *Shekinah*, or divine presence, manifested itself wherever a *minyan* was formed. Through prayer the Jews could welcome Yahweh in their midst again, wherever they might be, scattered across the continents.

Thus the synagogue represented a continuum with the Temple. It was the nearest the people had to a link with God. So, when the Black Jews were told by the Paradesis that they were not equal in the synagogue, it was a rejection that struck at their very core.

*

Rabbi ibn Zimra's edict in 1520 marked the first tentative step towards equality. The rabbi had ruled that the Black Jews did have the right to intermarry and enter the synagogue as equals, provided all the proper conversion rituals had taken place. But the Paradesi leaders refused to budge and ignored the foreign rabbi's ruling. A generation later, the Black Jews renewed their campaign in another letter, which was dispatched to a former student of ibn Zimra, Rabbi Jacob de Castro in Alexandria. After studying his teacher's earlier missives, he reiterated that equality and marriage between the two groups was permissible. But again, the Paradesi Jews simply ignored the letter.

On the face of it, discrimination was targeted at the so-called *meshuchrarim*, or 'manumitted ones', former slaves who had been freed by their Jewish masters. In reality, though, the slave tag was used by the Whites to refer to anyone in the synagogue community they deemed to be non-white. The slur of slavery continued long after the British abolished the practice.

In the eighteenth century the Paradesis said their congregation did not recognize as equals children born from unions between white men and non-white women. According to Katz and Goldberg, a 1757 entry in the Record Book of the Paradesi Synagogue sets the position out clearly:

> If an Israelite or Ger (convert) marries a woman from the daughters of the Black Jews or the daughters of the *meshuchrarim* (manumitted slaves), the sons born to them go after the mother; but the man, the Israelite or Ger, he stands in the congregation of our community and he has no blemish.

There were eight synagogues across Cochin, seven of which were used by the Black Jews. The eighth synagogue, the Paradesi, was a bastion of white purity. Any Black Jews who lived close to it faced a ferocious battle for access. For almost four centuries, the Blacks were denied entry to the synagogue, denied the right to perform rituals there, banned from chanting certain liturgical hymns, banned from reading the Torah or scriptures, and prohibited from marrying into White Jewish families. These were seen as polluting acts which could taint

the purity of the Paradesi community. Black families were barred from burying their dead in coffins or in the Paradesi Synagogue cemetery a few hundred metres away. In worship, love and even death, the colour of a Jew's skin determined his destiny. All these prohibitions directly flouted Jewish law.

The Black Jews fought the discrimination one issue at a time. But the seminal battle was for equality in faith. During the centuries when Mattancheri's Black Jews were not allowed to sit on the benches of the Paradesi Synagogue, they were relegated to sitting on the dirt floor of the anteroom. From this lowly position they could hear services conducted by the White community. Many foreign observers found it shocking. Claudius Buchanan, a missionary who visited Cochin between 1806 and 1808, wrote that 'It is only necessary to look at the countenance of the Black Jews to be satisfied that their ancestors must have arrived in India many ages before the White Jews.' He then added that despite this lineage, 'The White Jews look upon the Black Jews as an inferior race and as not of a pure caste.'

A modern-day observer, Rabbi Louis Rabinowitz, writes in *Far East Mission* that in Cochin 'irrational prejudices take precedence over law and logic and ethics'. He drew parallels with South African apartheid, in that White Jews were the dominant section of society even though they were a minority – they represented one third of the local congregation in Mattancheri. If the segregation was ever challenged by the Blacks, the Whites would call upon the raja or local colonial powers to intervene on their behalf and quell any resistance.

The Blacks tried hard to challenge the discrimination in the synagogue. Katz and Goldberg say that a number of visiting foreign Jews also lobbied on the Blacks' behalf for equality, but to no avail. By 1840 the Blacks found their situation intolerable and relations had reached a point where something had to give. Either the Whites must end the discrimination or the Blacks would rebel. In the end, it was rebellion.

The Blacks escalated the pressure on the Whites and the protestors were ejected from the synagogue community. Barred from worship even in the Paradesi Synagogue ante-room, some of the Black Jews asked for permission to establish their own place of worship in one of the homes in Jew Town. The White leaders refused even this compromise. Following one particularly acrimonious exchange, the Whites enlisted the support of the local diwan, who decreed that no prayer services should be conducted by 'the group with impurity in the house appropriated for that purpose', according to Johnson's *Our Community in Two Worlds*. As a further insult, the Blacks were instructed by the diwan to 'walk submissively' before the White Jews, by way of contrition.

The 'group with impurity' was led by a Black Jew called Avraham, or Avo, Hallegua, the grandfather of A. B. Salem. Who was Avo? One version of his history says that he was the son of a rich landowner, Shlomo Hallegua, and a woman named Hannah, who was either born a slave or was the descendant of a poor foreign Jewish family. Either way, Hannah's Jewish credentials were deemed dubious and not

acceptable to the White community. Therefore the marriage of Shlomo Hallegua and Hannah was not conducted in the synagogue but took place at his grand estate in Vettacka.

They conceived a son and Avo was born and grew up on the Hallegua estate. During this time, according to a document of manumission, Hannah was freed on the eve of Passover in 1826, with a stipulation that her sons be counted in the *minyan*. This should have cleansed her of the past and accorded her offspring full rights in the synagogue. After this key event, Avo was given a full Jewish education and schooled in the teachings of the Torah.

But even a wealthy landowner like Hallegua was not impervious to the pressure of his peers. He was urged to marry a White Jewess. He did so, and she also bore a son. When Hallegua died, Avo took over the estate and managed the business single-handed as his half brother was still a child. But once the child reached adulthood, the old order reasserted itself. The younger brother, a White Jew, barred his brother from the ancestral estate and took his share of the inheritance. The Paradesis rallied around the younger brother as the dispute became steeped in bitterness. In the end, the matter was taken before the Cochini raja, who ruled in favour of the White brother.

Avo lost everything. He was barred from his home and denied his share in the family estate which he had run since his father died. Overnight, he had become an outcast. Such a brutal rejection would have broken most men. But Avo was unlike others. He channelled his anger over his stolen birthright

into a broader campaign: to take on the Paradesis directly, not over inheritance or land, but over the religious rights that had been denied to Black Jews like him for centuries. In his view, this was the most unforgivable of all the humiliations suffered by his people. The idea that the Blacks were somehow lesser Jews than Whites was the poisoned source from which all iniquity sprang. In so doing, Avo rose from being a disenfranchised landowner to become Cochin's first Black Jewish civil-rights leader.

After the Blacks were banned from having their own separate synagogue in Mattancheri's Jew Town, a group left and resettled in the British territory of Fort Cochin, a short distance away. There, they turned a private house into a synagogue and Avo took on the role of religious scribe, or *sofer*, as well as *shohet*. At first, their new community was successful. The resettled Black Jews thrived and were integrated into the local community. They got on well with their non-Jewish neighbours and reports of those times show that the Black Jews were well-to-do. The Jewish women sported gold jewellery and their households employed servants. Their revived fortunes contrasted sharply with their old rivals, the Paradesis, who were by 1830 less well off.

But the Black Jews' good fortune proved to be short-lived, as disaster struck Fort Cochin. A cholera epidemic swept through their neighbourhood and most of their number was wiped out in a matter of days. The few that survived left for Bombay or Calcutta, where there were other Jewish communities, or returned to Mattancheri's Jew Town.

The Paradesi leaders revelled in the misfortune of those who came back. They were told that if they wished to return to their lowly position on the floor of the synagogue anteroom, they would have to pay a fine before being rehabilitated. The Whites saw the defection to Fort Cochin as an act of blasphemy and insurrection. One of the Whites was a man called Reinman, who wrote about the whole sorry affair in '*Masa'oth Shlomo b'Kogin*'. He was actually fairly sympathetic, unlike some of the others, yet even he believed the Blacks had courted catastrophe through their ill-conceived defiance:

> God punished the sin of the [Blacks] who were disloyal and withdrew from the synagogue of the White Jews and desecrated its holiness... almost all of [them] died with the plague and epidemic... and many who remained became mad and got out of hand. The remainder of the refugees turned to the White Jews and paid a fine to the synagogue to accept them as before. Avo... died naked and for want of everything and his only son went out of his mind.

That last line on the fate of Avo would have been a heart-breaking epitaph if it had been the end of the matter. But it was not. Avo's true legacy was that he imbued a spirit of change in his people. That spirit remained undiminished even with his death.

In 1882 the Black Jews again asked the diwan to permit them to worship in a private house. They sought the help of David Sassoon, the Bombay businessman, who wrote to the

British Resident on their behalf. Again the plea failed. Disappointed and rejected, all they could do was keep going.

News continued to spread to the Jewish community overseas of the discrimination practised by Cochin's Jewry. Rabbinical emissaries from Jerusalem arrived in India to resolve the problem. As had happened three hundred years earlier, the chief rabbi of Jerusalem, Rabbi Phanizel, ruled in 1882 that the so-called slaves should enjoy full religious privileges provided the special conversion ceremony was carried out. History repeated itself as the Paradesis again defied the rabbi's ruling. It seemed even the highest authorities could not force the Whites to recognize the Blacks' rights.

It would take the grandson and namesake of Avo to force the change. Where rabbis, elders and foreign emissaries failed, a low-born black lawyer from Ernakulam, A. B. Salem, would succeed. What Avo started, his grandson would finish in the following century.

With his birthright stolen, Salem did not have riches at his disposal, nor vast estates or privilege. But he did inherit his grandfather's indomitable spirit and he was fired by the same zeal for justice. He used his law degree to fight the cases of the oppressed, not just for fellow Jews, but for the lowest sections of society. For example, through the organization of trade unions, he helped low-paid workers such as the boatmen to improve their rights at work.

Salem's interest in grass-root politics eventually elevated him into the upper echelons of Cochini society and he served on the Cochin Legislative Assembly. In 1929 he was a delegate

of the native Princely States of Cochin and Travancore to the National Congress meeting in Lahore where Gandhi launched his struggle for independence.

This was a turning point in Cochini Jewish history, as it was for Indian nationalism generally. It was here that Salem was converted to the gospel of Gandhian non-violent protest. He decided that if Indians could fight even the military might of the British using such methods, the Black Jews could deploy this same weapon in their struggle for equality in the synagogue.

Gandhi had used the tactic of passive resistance to campaign successfully on behalf of the Untouchables in neighbouring Travancore. The Untouchables, now known as Dalits, were at the bottom of the Hindu caste system, had minimal rights and were ruthlessly exploited by the upper castes. On his return from the congress, an inspired Salem organized a *satyagraha*, or non-violent resistance, in the synagogue. He agreed with Gandhi that religious discrimination was 'most pernicious' and was determined to end it in his own backyard.

Just as Gandhi's empowerment through peace led to a mass political awakening in India, so the 'Jewish Gandhi' also succeeded in his small-town revolution. The overturning of a tainted history began with one man staging sit-ins at the synagogue, using his oratory to advocate change and even, at one stage, threatening to fast until death. Salem recruited his young sons – Raymond, Balfour and Gamy – to the cause, even though they were still small children. He would take his

sons to the synagogue and refuse to sit in the designated space for the Blacks on the anteroom floor. Shunning this lowly position, he defiantly strode into the main synagogue itself, dragging his sons behind him.

One man who knew Salem in those heady days of protest was the father of Isaac Joshua, who is the current president of the Association of Kerala Jews and managing trustee of the Ernakulam Synagogue. Isaac, the foremost elder among the Cochini Jews, now in his mid-eighties, had grown up with his father's accounts of the Jewish Gandhi, who was a close family friend. 'I remember him too well,' Isaac told me, scratching his shiny copper-coloured pate. 'He used to come to our house and synagogue for service and then he came for lunch every Saturday and spent Sabbath with us. He was my father's great friend.

'In those days before the change, the Blacks were forced to sit on the ground outside. Well, Salem wasn't going to take it any longer!' The old man's eyes sparked as he recalled Salem's audacious plan.

'He started by sitting under the windowsill, looking into the synagogue. Then *on* the sill. Body was on the sill, but his legs were technically outside. That's how it began. Slowly, he put one leg inside, then the other. These people had no guts to stop him. Then slowly, he came inside and sat there, and so it went on. They couldn't stop him.' He shook his head as he laughed and wagged his finger. 'They couldn't stop this man, they simply looked daggers. He then started taking his sons with him. He was a very strong man and they were scared. He

was a top lawyer, a writer, he knew Gandhi, he knew Nehru. Salem was our Jewish Gandhi.'

Salem did not stop there. He wanted every Jew to have access to the Paradesi Synagogue, the weak as well as the strong. He held full prayer services at his home or joined the prayers at the homes of other Blacks who could withstand the humiliation of the synagogue apartheid no longer. Through such small acts of defiance, Salem effected great change. He skilfully articulated the Black cause, combining his devastating lawyer's logic with a rousing oratory that began to sway younger, more modern thinking members of the Paradesi community. A small number of Whites became convinced that segregation was wrong.

These younger, progressive Whites joined Salem's campaign for change and their support proved to be the tipping point which would lead to a revolution on Synagogue Lane. Inspired by Salem, young White Jewish men used their own methods of non-violent protest. They refused to carry the heavy Torah scrolls during the Simhat Torah processions until change was introduced. Their revolt led to a breakthrough – eventually two benches were set up for the Blacks at the back of the Paradesi Synagogue. They were just two small benches at the back, but for the first time in four hundred years, the Black Jews were *inside*. They had moved from the floor of the anteroom to the heart of religious proceedings. In 1937 the academic and long-time observer of the community, David Mandelbaum, visited the synagogue and reported an astonishing change: Blacks could read

from the Law on weekdays, although not on Sabbath.

Still Salem was not satisfied. Blessed with formidable patience as well as a ferocious intellect, he relentlessly chipped away at the edifice of prejudice, piece by piece, until it came tumbling down. In 1942 he recorded in his journal:

[For the first time in the History of the Paradesi Synagogue I got the chance, by stressing the law of the religious services regarding the reading of Torah, the privilege of reading the Maphtir of this Sabbath and Rosh Hodesh. May God be praised... May the innovation become the order of the day!

This was the closest the understated Salem got to trumpeting Black Jewish religious emancipation. Yet his exclamation mark at the end of that sentence speaks as clearly as any victory speech of the joy that must have overwhelmed his heart that day. It was just the beginning, as he envisaged. By the close of the decade, there were further landmarks on the road to equality. The Blacks could bury their dead in a separate area of the Paradesi Synagogue cemetery. Blacks and Whites were still not allowed to lie side by side in death, but at least now they could share the same soil. But, most important of all, Black Jews could be called to read Torah on Sabbath and recite blessings.

Yet there was still a way to go. Blacks were barred from holding weddings or circumcisions in the Paradesi Synagogue. These had to be conducted at home. Also, marriage between Black and White was still prohibited.

The coming decade would see great changes in Cochin's Jew Town and for Jews worldwide. The birth of the state of Israel in 1948 triggered a wave of mass migration of Jews everywhere. The founding fathers of Israel wished to create a rainbow nation, where the Diaspora of Jews of every hue and nationality could reunite in their ancient land once more. The idea of Jews of every colour coming together to summon up a nation state from the desert sands no doubt inspired further change among the Black and White Jews of Cochin. After all, in the motherland itself every Jew – regardless of colour – played an equal part in nation-building.

Within a few years of the creation of Israel and the Blacks winning equality in the Paradesi Synagogue, the last taboo was broken by a passionate affair between two young lovers, Balfour and Baby. Their love is the final chapter in the story of apartheid in Cochin's Jew Town. It took Salem's oldest son and his beautiful and spirited bride to bring the era of segregation to a close. Theirs was a final conflict between love and prejudice. And as in all great romances, prejudice was vanquished. Love won.

Nine

Taboo Love

'My dove, your splendour resembles Orion and the
   Pleiades
And I, for love of you, shall sing a song.'

Sixteenth-century poem by Israel Moses Najara,
sung by Cochini Jews

Wedding fever had gripped Synagogue Lane. A flutter of creamy manila envelopes arrived in the post, pronouncing the forthcoming nuptials of the young couple. On hearing the news, for a moment I envisioned some Hollywood-style ending, a sigh-inducing rapprochement in the long-running saga of Yaheh and Keith. Had cold indifference given way to slow-burning pragmatism? Had the elders finally bent them into submission, or had they decided over too many glasses of 'petrol' toddy that they would sacrifice themselves to save thousands of years of history after all?

   'Don't be a damned fool,' said Gamy, as if I'd suggested sun and moon could dance in the same sky. 'Balfour and

Baby's grandson is getting married in Israel. A nice Jewish girl. Reema, Sammy and Queenie fly out in a few days.'

The wedding would be held near Haifa, close to where Baby continued to live after her husband died. There would be no wedding ceremony in Cochin – the last one had taken place generations ago. Still, a wedding was a wedding, and if the couple would not come to Cochin, then a banquet would be held in their honour.

The news had the desired effect: the Paradesis walked around with smiles on their faces and it was good to see. A wedding was a time to rejoice and forget the past few weeks with the burial of Shalom, the stress of organizing the festival season, and indeed to forget the difficulties of the past years. Those attending the wedding were in a whirlwind of preparation and those remaining in Mattancheri were planning the finest party Jew Town had seen in a while. The couple would be toasted from Israel to India.

'Since your Enemy Number One is flying to Israel,' suggested Gamy, 'you shall come to the party. Johnny's house, Wednesday, eight o'clock. Just don't tell Sammy.'

Sammy, Queenie and Reema would be flying to Mumbai, where they would change flights for Israel. Gamy had already been in touch with Indian Airlines and El Al to arrange for wheelchairs to take them through check-in and security. The three of them would need an additional entourage of porters to deal with the accompanying luggage. I watched in bafflement as Gamy, Reema and old Mary grappled with a dusty brown

leather suitcase that had been hauled out of storage for the occasion, and began to pack.

It was the arduous task known to every Indian family, Jewish or not. I had learned from my own family that Indians never travel light. The concept of capsule packing is unknown in the subcontinent. Even the shortest of trips required certain essentials: a choice of heirloom jewellery for parties, gifts for the elders, mangos by the box-load, one small bag of superior-quality chapatti flour, one kilo each of garam masala, cumin and coriander seeds, chocolate and toys for all the children. And pickle.

Gamy deliberated briefly over whether the family in Haifa would require dried fish as well, or whether pickle was an adequate condiment option. The packing naturally took days to complete. At one stage Gamy could be seen throwing small Indian dolls across the parlour floor, raging that he had specifically requested small, easy-to-pack toys, not full-size action heroes. The night before departure the brown suitcase sat in the entrance hall, straining at its zip like a squat Indian gentleman suffering from explosive indigestion after too much butter chicken. For the first time in my life, I pitied the immigration customs officers at Ben Gurion International Airport. They would need a bigger table.

*

Sammy, Queenie, Reema and her suitcase of never-ending treasures departed for Israel. As their white Ambassador taxi

disappeared from view, Gamy had a look on his face which said, 'Let the drinking commence.' The men quickly got down to doing what men do best – they carefully judged the amount of whisky that needed to be purchased and consumed that evening. Did the occasion merit just plain Indian whisky or should a bottle of Johnny Walker Black Label be procured? Such weighty debates went on late into the afternoon. Meanwhile, the women got together, jotted down a menu, shopped and then cooked up a storm under the leadership of Johnny's wife, Juliette, who was widely acknowledged as the best cook on Synagogue Lane.

The party was to be held at their house, the Hallegua mansion right at the top of Synagogue Lane. Johnny insisted that as the senior elder in Jew Town after Sammy had left, he would take care of the celebrations. He refused to accept payment or help and Gamy was grateful, as it was certainly a cost he could ill afford. Everyone was invited. The last Jews of Kerala would gather that evening to celebrate the wedding of the grandson of Baby and Balfour, the first couple to unite the two communities. The only one not to attend was Sarah, who was still in mourning for Shalom. Even so she would not miss out on the feast, as Juliette had arranged to send her a plate of food. Without the solemn presence of the patriarch, the mood became light, almost frivolous. Then just before sundown everyone disappeared into their houses to say evening prayers and get ready.

As I approached the Hallegua mansion that evening, it was unnaturally quiet. I knocked at the door and it opened a

crack; just a sliver of light and one eye was visible. It was Yaheh, who looked surprised to see me. She had that stern look on her face again.

'Hi, I'm here for the party.'

'What party?'

'The wedding party.'

'What wedding?'

She was good. She didn't even blink. In a parallel universe she would have been the poker player in Vegas with the most sangfroid. I could imagine her celebrating in the bar after breaking the house, taking to the stage and belting out Bette Midler show tunes.

'Your father and Gamy invited me.'

The door closed. A minute passed, then it swung wide open and the doorway was suddenly flooded with yellow light. Conviviality and the distant sound of singing from the back of the house reached me. Yaheh smiled broadly. Not a fake, tight smile, but a real beam, full of pleasure.

'Come in. You're very welcome in our house. Let me take you through.'

She was transformed by the occasion: not just in demeanour but in appearance too; she was wearing light make-up, her lipstick-mouth like a summer strawberry, and was dressed in a rainbow silk kaftan that rippled colour as she moved. She led me through the old house, suddenly effusive with pride and hospitality. The entrance parlour was a grand room with dizzily high ceilings and wonderful mosaic floors made for waltzing. Antique carved furniture adorned the room and a

television set buzzed away in the corner as some of the young men from Ernakulam watched the cricket, periodically shrieking with delight. The house was almost three hundred years old and much of its original character was unchanged. The cracked plaster walls breathed memories of the past sorrows and celebrations of the White Jews and I wished I could discern their secrets. From the salon we walked through to a long corridor. Seated on a pew along one wall were the ladies, all attired in their finest outfits, primped and pretty as if waiting to be asked to dance.

The aunties cooed their welcome as Yaheh introduced me. Most of them I already knew. The older ladies wore embroidered chiffon saris in the colours of Kerala: petrol blue, lime green, dusty pink. Gold bangles jangled on their arms as they carefully smoothed down their dark hair, polished and perfumed with coconut oil. Dangling earrings swung from their ears as they turned their heads in conversation, and many wore the traditional Jewish wedding necklace. There were just a couple of young girls from Ernakulam, shy and awkward, in trendy westernized clothes, sipping cola and squirming with displeasure as their mothers fussed over them. Juliette and Yaheh ran the proceedings with effortless aplomb, keeping the conversation, food and drink flowing. The table opposite was laden with sodas for the ladies, whisky, beer and rum for the men, who were all gathered in the dining room to the left of the corridor. Raucous laughter and a hybrid of Malayalam and Hebrew burst from the open doorway, punctuated by quavering snatches of old Jewish songs. They sang of love, of marriage.

A slightly tipsy Gamy tottered over. His glasses had slipped down his nose and his long front teeth seemed to have lengthened under the influence of alcohol. Armed with a Coke, he led me into the dining room, where I sat next to him, Johnny and Isaac Joshua from Ernakulam. By the look of them all, either I was very late or they had started very early. Around thirty men, Black and White, Indian and foreign guests, sat round the huge table that was used for formal banquets. A Star of David light twinkled on the wall opposite. The men started another round of singing, thumping the table as they sang, each trying to outdo the other. Even the gentle Isaac Ashkenazy joined in, never happier than when he was surrounded by rowdy male company and safe from the perils of predatory females. In the absence of Sammy, Isaac Joshua led the festivities. In a room full of voices, his bellowed the loudest.

The ladies flitted in and out, bearing great platters of hot food, a fabulous spread of tongue-lashing chilli chicken curry, delicately spiced kidneys with onion, tomato and finely chopped *dhania*, rice, salads, pastels and pickles. In the name of a couple far away, a couple most had never met, they united in celebration. Isaac ordered a replenishment of plates and glasses. Then in the soft haze of satisfaction, it was time for the community to offer prayers for the couple. Unsteadily he rose to his feet, passed his hand over his bald head as if for good luck, and began to read from the Torah, voice trembling with the melody of its meaning. His audience was overcome; a couple of the men snuffled into their hankies. It cannot have

escaped them that this was a wedding that should have taken place in Cochin and that there would never be another wedding on this street in their lifetime or their children's. Isaac led the prayers for more than thirty minutes. Gamy, ever provocative, said he couldn't remember all the words, only to receive a look of severe remonstrance from Isaac which was enough to subdue him. For this was the nature of family: united in a tumultuous shared history, yet distinct in nature and temperament; rousing camaraderie one minute and irritating the hell out of one another the next; capable of love despite having hurt one another. For the first time since I arrived in Cochin, that night around Johnny and Juliette's table the Black and White Jews were one, grievances forsaken like false lovers and the past a forgotten territory. There could be no better wedding gift for a young couple in Israel.

*

As the men sang late into the night, the women remembered weddings past. They were no different to womenfolk of any community: talk centred on what outfit the bride might wear, the ceremony and love songs. I looked at Juliette, who was happy that the party had been a success, cheeks flushed with pleasure. Her daughter Yaheh also seemed very much at peace as she gently stroked Baby Doll's fur and laughed with the others. Keith had not come that night, nor his brother Len. Pretty much everyone else was there, but they remained the invisible men of Synagogue Lane.

In the old days marriages were arranged and there was little say in the matter for the youngsters. That was the Indian as well as the Jewish way. Once the bride's family had received a proposal and accepted, the people of Jew Town would gather and summon the couple. The foremost elder would ask the groom if the match met his parents' wishes and then he would ask the young man's own wish, to which he replied simply: 'I desire her.'

Once the engagement was toasted, the women would bake sesame cookies as a symbol of fertility and a wedding date was fixed. In the community's heyday, the bridal outfit of the Cochini Jews was known for its exceptional finery. The fabric for the bride's skirt was silk lined with cotton, stretched tight on a wooden frame and hand embroidered by the Muslim dressmakers who were known for their intricate needlework. The wedding blouse was sheer white muslin, edged with gold, and upon her head she would wear a cap decorated with more gold jewellery or embroidery. Around her neck she wore the kali mala, a heavy beaded necklace made up of pearls or gold coins or sometimes squares of turtle shell. Before the wedding, the local goldsmith would come to the bridal home and in the presence of the couple and their families he would fashion the ring from a gold coin provided by the groom's father. The traditional Hindu bridal necklace, the tali mala, made of gold and inlaid gems, was then clasped around the bride's neck by the groom's sister. This was one Hindu custom that the Kerala Jews adopted.

The road to the synagogue was spread with coconut

branches and men were hired to beat drums, while troupes of Hindu musicians played Jewish wedding songs. The Jews were just one of the many religions that had been woven into Kerala's multi-faith history. In Cochin, the Muslim would painstakingly sew the Jewish bride's blouse, while the Hindu would lend his music and song to her wedding procession.

The ceremony took place in the synagogue. Before the groom left his house a lump of sugar was placed in his mouth, so he might always taste the sweetness in life. He would arrive at the synagogue at the head of a procession with a parasol over his head or sometimes hoisted on the shoulders of friends, accompanied by whoops of joy, the rat-tat-tat of firecrackers and lighted torches. The groom was also dressed in white, with a gold-embroidered *kippah* and a garland of flowers around his neck. Years ago, the groom would be attired in a Baghdadi-style silk kaftan and white turban. At the synagogue he was received by guests who showered him with bright green leaves and tiny coins.

As he took his place on the *tevah*, the groom looked towards his bride and then recited a love song. Sometimes the congregation would join in. The bride sat on a chair, screened from view by a linen curtain on a circular rail above her head. On the table in front of the Ark was the *ketubah*, the synagogue registry, pen and inkstand. The Cochini *ketubah*, or marriage contract, is quite beautiful, lavishly decorated with flowers, birds of paradise and animals as well as auspicious motifs around a central inscription calling upon God to bless the marriage and make it fertile: 'Your wife shall be like a fruitful

vine within your house; your sons like olive saplings around your table. So shall the man who fears the Lord be blessed.'

As happy memories flooded the Hallegua household, I heard the love story of the grandparents of the groom we were toasting. 'Now that was something,' said one of the ladies softly as she smoothed the skirts of her sari. 'Baby and Balfour went through so much to be together. See, they were what you people would call a love match.'

*

The year was 1950, the era of conservatism, not just in India but in the West. India was newly independent, yet entrenched in the ancient social traditions and caste boundaries. America's civil-rights movement was still nascent; Britain was about to witness seismic changes to its cultural landscape as children of the Empire arrived to make a new life. And the Black Jews of Kerala, who had been early pioneers in their battle for racial equality since the sixteenth century, would begin the 1950s by breaking the last taboo among Black and White Jews.

Balfour was the second son of Ruth and A. B. Salem, the man who did more than anyone to break down the barriers between the Paradesi and Malabari Jews. Balfour was the one who fought for equality in matters of the heart. A tall man, with slick black hair and a neat pencil moustache in the style of a silent-movie star, he fell in love with Seema 'Baby' Koder, who belonged to the White community. She bore the name of

one of the great Paradesi clans and she was also a beauty, with expressive dark eyes and a creamy complexion. Baby and Balfour decided they would marry but were coldly informed by the White elders that their marriage could not be held in the Paradesi Synagogue.

Undeterred, they left for Bombay, where they married in a Baghdadi Jewish synagogue with only A. B. Salem and his oldest son Raymond in attendance. The bride's family refused to come and the wedding was boycotted by other Cochini Jews who had migrated to Bombay. Their love affair was deemed a scandal; it flouted centuries of tradition that decreed that Black and White Jews should never intermarry.

Raymond took the official wedding photograph of the couple. It shows Balfour dressed in a smart white double-breasted suit, with dark cravat and pocket handkerchief and white loafers, looking every inch the sophisticated dandy. A small smile played beneath his moustache as he lent an arm to his bride. Baby wore an ornate lace gown, with a long tulle train. Her hair was pulled back into a loose chignon and held in place with a headpiece of white flowers and lace. Cradled in her arms was a bouquet of white flowers and palm fronds to remind her of home. She was perfect, yet it was not her vestal beauty that struck me while examining the old photo, but the look of defiance written in the soft curves of her face. As if she knew what was coming.

Back in Cochin, the elders reacted with utter disbelief and rage. Keen to scupper the union, a visiting rabbi was consulted on the legality of the marriage, but he harked back to the

sixteenth-century rabbinical ruling which said marriage was permissible provided all the proper ceremonies had been carried out.

The couple initially moved to Madras, in the neighbouring state of Tamil Nadu. Balfour got work as an engineer there and Baby attempted to broker reconciliation with her family through a series of letters. Her family rejected her entreaties. Indeed, the rest of her community decided that if she ever set foot in Cochin, she should be barred from the Paradesi Synagogue.

As months passed the pain of separation became intolerable. The couple were displaced from their family, their synagogue and yearned to come home. Baby's parents were also missing their daughter, and with the approach of Yom Kippur, they relented and invited her to visit.

It should have been a happy homecoming. But Baby did not know that the Paradesi elders had passed a motion to bar her from entering the synagogue. As far as they were concerned, she was no longer a White Jew, she was a person of no status in their eyes. She arrived in time for Yom Kippur but was told by her family and in-laws to avoid the synagogue. The Paradesi elders had already decided that if she arrived to pray, they would stage a walkout and hold services in Sassoon Hall, a private house a few doors down. Some of the Torah scrolls had already been taken there in preparation.

Many would have found such a boycott difficult to bear. But the steely look in Baby's eye hinted she was tougher than anyone imagined. On the day of Shabbat, she walked boldly

into the Paradesi Synagogue to take her place upstairs. There was an immediate walkout of both men and women, while one man ordered her to leave. These were people she had grown up with, so their rejection must have cut deep. Her resolve undiminished, she remained in her seat, insisting on her right to pray in the synagogue. They left her to it, unwilling to share the synagogue with what they saw as a tarnished woman. Only when she had finished praying did Baby get up from her seat and leave. It was the Kerala Jews' Rosa Parks moment.

Baby stood by her principles. Yet for the sake of harmony and perhaps her family, when she visited the Paradesi Synagogue in the future, she did not go upstairs, but sat on a bench downstairs at the back. In old age, she confided to friends and family the loneliness of those first days of married life and her return to Kerala. After some time the couple relocated to Cochin and many families continued to cut them out of their society. The pettiness of some of her neighbours was vicious, with a few families even refusing to attend any party that Balfour and Baby were invited to. Yet some did accept the marriage and over time life almost returned to normality.

The Salems continued to trail-blaze. Where Balfour went, his younger brother Gamy followed. Gamy and Reema married seven years later in Bombay. But when it came to going to synagogue, Reema simply took a seat downstairs and at the back, explaining that she did not have her sister-in-law's pugnacious spirit.

One account of the story, *Kashrut, Caste and Kabballah*

by Katz and Goldberg, tells how the young Gamy was so angered by the discrimination of the elders that he boycotted synagogue services for many years. To this day Gamy seemed to have little love for religion, having suffered at first hand the bigotry that was practised in its name. His sisters went further, marrying outside the Jewish community altogether. Esther married a Hindu and Malkah a Christian.

The prejudice continued to plague the following generation. Baby and Balfour's first son Leslie was banned from being circumcised in the synagogue itself because he was of mixed blood. Instead, the Paradesi elders suggested the ritual take place in Sassoon Hall. The couple was incensed at the suggestion that the ceremony be held in a private house and instead chose to have him circumcised in one of the Malabari synagogues. The stubborn Paradesi elders refused to acknowledge this alternative arrangement and, like characters in some black comedy, they remained seated in silence in Sassoon Hall, hosting a circumcision banquet in the absence of the child and his parents.

It took a generation for equality to arrive in matters of love. When Leslie grew up and married Glennis Simon, another White Jewess, things had moved on considerably from the time of his parents' wedding. Everyone, Black and White, came to celebrate the marriage in 1978. The last taboo had been irrevocably destroyed.

But by then it was too late to make any difference to the community's future. After millennia of Jewish refugees coming to Kerala's shores, the tide of migration had turned back

towards Israel. Within a decade or so, most of the community was gone. Balfour, Baby, Leslie and Glennis were among those who moved to Israel. Balfour died there but Baby lived to see her grandson's wedding day in the land of their forefathers. Their way turned out to be the future. All Jews coming together: this was what Israel was meant to be. The time of the old Paradesi prejudices was over. Yet the taste of victory was bitter upon their lips.

Ten

'A Wife Who Will Not Give Me Headache'

'My rabbi said, "Settle, settle. What about a woman like Mrs Blitzstein? She may not be a great beauty, but nobody is better at smuggling food and light firearms in and out of the ghetto..." Pity my dilemma, dear reader. Never to find all the requirements one needs in a single member of the opposite sex.'

Woody Allen, *Complete Prose*

After the exodus from Kerala, those left behind faced stark choices, particularly the few youngsters that remained. There were no people in their teens or twenties in the Paradesi community, but among the Malabaris there were some: Babu's girls, another three daughters in the old Jewish village of Parul and the Abraham boys, Anil and Solomon.

Solomon had already left Cochin for Chennai, where he worked. At the wedding celebration at Johnny's house, Anil

and his brother spent most of the night watching cricket, whooping with delight, but later that evening as we chatted he offered to take me around Cochin the next day to show me the old villages of Parul and Chennamangalam.

Anil was the eldest son of Samuel Abraham, who had moved to Israel before coming home again, disenchanted with what he discovered there. Anil's maternal grandfather was the leading elder of the Malabari Jews, Isaac Joshua, who was fiercely protective of his community's legacy. Anil grew up in the heart of this influential family, built on devotion to one another and to the faith. At the Simhat Torah celebration a few evenings before, I had met Anil for the first time. While the Paradesi Synagogue had been dressed for the occasion and dazzled, the Ernakulam place of worship was simply lit and furnished with a few garlands of fresh jasmine. In some ways it reflected the character of the communities themselves. That night I watched a young man who had inherited his grandfather's great seriousness and sense of purpose combined with an ability to find humour in everything. He was a natural optimist and seemed to infect everyone with his easy manner. Anil had the potential to take over from Isaac Joshua, I thought, if there was anything left to lead by that time. After the prayer ceremony, Anil had assisted his grandfather and father in preparing for the blessings at the dinner table before we sat down to a Simhat Torah feast for the Malabaris and their friends. There were forty of us – Jews and non-Jews – around the table. Here, Anil was at his most contented – in the synagogue anteroom, eating fire-breathing curry, singing

old Hebrew songs as his raucous grandfather thumped the table to keep time. After a few drinks, as everyone melted into conviviality, he would cast a shy glance towards the girls at the other end of the table, slowly passing a hand over his hair, smoothing it down.

Over the years the family had constructed a very happy and comfortable life in a suburb near Ernakulam. They had a successful business now and Anil was working as a tour guide. It earned him top dollar rates and the only thing left was to find a wife and settle down.

In any other society his options would be good. He was in his late twenties, from a respectable family and with a well-paid job. His two biggest attributes were his likeability and his integrity. He had lived part of his childhood in Israel until the family came back. Unlike many others, Anil had no desire to leave India again. His heart was bound to Kerala. As we walked along the riverbank not far from the historic Jewish village of Parul, he told me of his dilemma. He loved it here. The food, the people, the land. The smell of pepper, which grew in long curling strands on the trees all around us. Walking through ankle-deep grass along the riverbanks, shaded by tall slender palms and pepper trees. Watching the narrow-boats dotting the river, as fishermen draw nets like water-spangled cobwebs from the water. When Anil felt pressured, 'when I need to breathe', as he put it, he would climb into his car and drive for thirty minutes to a spot like this, where little had changed in a hundred years. He stretched out his hand and snatched a strand of green peppercorns

from a nearby tree. It lay in his palm like a tiny beaded necklace.

Anil was truly a man of Cochin. In a world where everyone seemed to want more, he told me he had enough. Nothing could match what he had been born to. And yet he was seriously considering going to Israel to find a bride. It was all that was missing. I asked him about the prospects for marriage here and he shook his head, rubbing the peppercorn necklace between finger and thumb, the friction releasing the pungent smell from the small green beads. His family had exhausted all options, not just in Kerala, where they were few, but even in Bombay, which was home to the Bene Israel Jews.

'I don't wish to go, you understand. But I must look at my choices. Here there's no chance to find a wife.'

When I asked him what he looked for in a bride, he didn't say she must be pretty, or rich or educated. His requirements were fairly uncomplicated.

'I wish for a Jewish wife who will not give me headache,' he said, and then laughed, as if embarrassed, as if he'd wished for the ridiculous.

*

He slipped the necklace into his pocket and we got back into the car to drive to the old Parul synagogue. Once it had been the most beautiful of all the eight places of worship in Kerala. The beautiful carved wooden Ark, engraved with flowers and leaves and topped with a crown, had been dismantled and

taken to the Israel Museum years ago. From the ceiling, as in the Paradesi Synagogue, there hung myriad glass lanterns of different colours. But the building was unsound and the Jews could not muster funds to save it. Anil hoped that by showing this to visiting Israelis and Jews from around the world, he could raise awareness and perhaps someone would offer to fund its restoration.

According to Jussay's *The Jews of Kerala*, Parul was the second-oldest synagogue after Cranganore, supposedly containing two Torah scrolls brought from Shingly after its destruction by the Moors. Jussay relates a story about how the synagogue fell into disuse after the Jews of Parul, angered by the Christians, offered incense in mockery of Christian worship. For this act of sacrilege, they were punished with the plague, he said. Their synagogue fell into disuse and the *ner tamid*, or Eternal Lamp, was hung in the street as a sign of contrition. It was rebuilt in 1616 by Jacob Castiel, leader of the Jewish community in Cochin.

The Parul Jews had further run-ins with some Christians who tried to disrupt their worship by loudly banging drums outside the synagogue during Shabbat. Frustrated, the Jews turned to the viceroy of India, who was visiting Travancore at the time. The Jews gained an audience with the viceroy, who was sympathetic and ordered two stone pillars to be built at the entrance to Jew Street to bar traffic. The Jews hailed this as a victory.

We pulled up outside Jew Street, just in front of its famous pillars. A white goat was tied to the synagogue's entrance

gates, which were locked. Anil went to talk to the neighbour, who warned him that the place had become infested with cobras and that there were so many they were infiltrating his house through the broken boundary walls.

We went to the gate and unlocked it. Lying between us and the synagogue itself was a vast, overgrown garden. The grass was almost waist-high in places, and brown and tangled bushes engulfed the pathway, which was no longer visible. If one looked carefully at the ground, one could discern pale gold translucent husks of old snake skins. The synagogue lay some fifty yards ahead. Nobody came here any more, so no one knew what state it was in. In a few years, with the entire community gone, would this be the fate of all the synagogues?

The goat bleated in fear, warning us not to go any further. Anil told me what the neighbours had said. 'They killed two cobras in the last week alone. Both came through the crack in the synagogue wall,' he said. Now the goat was pulling wildly at its tether, slipping and sliding as it attempted to move away from the gate. I wanted to see inside, but not enough to make that walk. 'If you're ready to meet your relatives and your maker, we can go see it,' joked Anil. 'I'm not quite ready yet, though.'

In the end we padlocked the gate again. Mightily relieved, the goat settled back into his spot and watched us leave. All the houses in Parul's Jew Town were now in the hands of Hindus and Christians. No Jews were left and the synagogue was the only reminder of what once was.

Anil now took me to meet his grandmother's brother, who lived not far from the other Jewish village of Chennamangalam, which had done much better in the lottery of preservation. It had won a grant from the Indian government to restore the synagogue. Next to the synagogue was the oldest Jewish tombstone in Kerala, dated 1269. It was inscribed in Hebrew with 'Sara bat Israel', or Sara, daughter of Israel. This was one of the oldest proofs of the antiquity of the Jewish community in Cochin. The synagogue's foundations were said to date back to the sixteenth century. But Chennamangalam had another claim to fame. It was also a symbol of religious tolerance. According to one story, a former maharajah wished to have each of the four major faiths represented in this place and so designated four points for the construction of a synagogue, a Christian church, a Hindu temple and a mosque. At the centre of these cardinal points, he built a palace. The four places of worship lie within one kilometre of one another and the locals claim it is the only village in the world where one can hear the shofar of the synagogue, the peel of the church bell, the trumpet of the Hindu conch shell and the cry of the muezzin.

Not far from here lived the brother of Anil's grandmother, the eighty-two-year-old Menachem, who was born in Chennamangalam itself. The house was set in a wild garden full of pepper, tamarind and fruit trees. Jackfruits and papaya lay strewn on the ground, a kitchen garden of herbs grew in fragrant profusion in a corner. Black chickens scuttled back and forth from shade to bush and back again as they made brief forays for titbits.

The house was newly renovated, with a porch and a tiled floor throughout. In the front parlour was an elaborately carved three-piece suite and a coffee table already laden with ladoos, deep-fried banana chips and other snacks, plus chai. The old man sat in an armchair. He had a fine head of grey hair and a strong, muscular physique apart from his right leg, which was withered after a childhood bout of polio. He tucked the leg back, hiding it from view beneath the folds of his lungi. Menachem spoke in a rapid, voluble manner, periodically stopping to laugh at his jokes as he wiped his eyes. He was charming and a born story teller, accompanying his tale with fearsome gesticulation.

I was here to listen to the story of a historic feud between Parul and Chennamangalam which stemmed from one of the most bizarre episodes in Kerala Jewish history. It was known as 'Sarah's story', and Sarah was a distant relative of Menachim, so who better to tell it? As I listened to the tale, I decided that Sarah would not have been Anil's kind of woman, being the kind of wife who induced not just 'headaches', but crippling migraines.

Sarah was a beautiful Jewess from a very wealthy land-owning family in Parul. At a very young age she married an equally rich man from a family in Chennamangalam, but was widowed a few years later after giving birth to two daughters. It was a difficult position for a young widow to be in. She was still young and very desirable, with the added complication that she was extremely rich. Her daughters would inherit a joint estate, which also made them targets for suitors.

Her late husband's family was keen to marry the daughters to their own young men, thereby securing the fortune. But Sarah's brothers demanded the same, so, apparently with the wisdom of Solomon, Sarah offered to give one daughter to Parul and the other to Chennamangalam. However, neither side was satisfied, so she incurred the wrath of both.

In a further attempt to gain control of her wealth, the relatives argued that Sarah was unfit to manage her money and offered to take control of her business affairs. But she was having none of it and decided to employ a poor Jew from Chennamangalam to assist her. She began to mix with people from all levels of society, further enraging the family, who claimed she was damaging her reputation.

Jussay wrote about the episode, which made the otherwise dry historian breathily report: 'They deliberately spread scandals about her. She was depicted as a shameless slut tarnishing the image of the entire Jewish community. Her own behaviour gave credence to these stories.' The historian seemed to have some sympathy with her relatives, adding reprovingly, 'She used to stay away from home for days together and used to welcome home visitors during odd hours.'

One of those visitors who stayed 'suspiciously long' was Thomman, a Christian leader from Gothuruth, a village of daring zealots who modelled themselves on the Red Cross Knights of Europe. Thomman and his friends formed their own Round Table of Knights, says Jussey, vowing to defend their faith with the sword and protect damsels in distress and

the like. This fabulous medieval-style religious intrigue took place in the midst of Kerala's tropical countryside just one hundred years ago.

So here was our heroine, the young, rich, gorgeous Jewish widow, refusing to deny herself any of life's pleasures to the horror of her male relatives. Thomman was everything they despised: a tall, athletic Christian with his own private posse. I asked Menachem about the relationship between Sarah and Thomman and the old man looked coy and blushed a little, so we shall have to turn to Jussay's version of events. 'The two became intimate,' he said delicately, and their behaviour sent the elders into a fury. The result was a boycott of Sarah.

But things got even more complicated. Sarah found out she was pregnant, although it is unclear by whom. She avoided scandal by marrying her footman. When the Jews of the two villages found out, their seething resentment boiled over into rage. They seized her unlucky husband and thrashed him by the riverside. A friend of Thomman found him and took care of him and then Thomman offered Sarah his protection and invited her to stay at his home where she would be safe.

Her life was now in danger and there were rumours that the Jewish elders would snatch her girls to save them from associated scandal. Sarah, her husband and the girls went to live with Thomman, her lover. This was too much for the Jewish elders, who gathered a group at Cochin, collected firearms and weapons and set out by rowboat to Gothuruth

to abduct the daughters and mother. Their plan was foiled when they were spotted by Thomman's brother, who raised the alarm.

Sarah ran to the rice-pounding shed and hid, the girls went upstairs and bolted the door to the room. The local Christians came to Sarah's aid, gathering makeshift weapons of poles, crowbars, choppers and spades. Menachem described how the attempted abduction failed:

'One of the brothers came inside. He was holding Sarah and trying to take her and the children forcibly. One Christian came in and told the brother to let go of her. The brother refused and said, "I'm taking her now." So the Christian chopped the brother's arm with a knife. After this, the Jews decided there should be no survivors and with their helpers they sealed all the exits to the village. One of my uncles was killed in this battle – my father's brother.'

Overpowered and outfoxed, the Jews fled to the boat but it was pulled ashore and smashed to pieces by the Christians. By now many men of the local village had returned from the bazaar and joined the fray, assailing the Jews in the water with blows from oars and poles. Disgraced and battered, the Jews were forced to retreat. The Jews turned to the courts for help but were rebuffed, because the court ruled the Christians acted in self-defence.

'A lot of people died,' said Menachem sadly. 'The people who came to take Sarah lost their fight. The Jews were jailed for two or three years. My father was also punished; he was just eighteen years old. It was a shameful case, to use force,'

said the old man, wrinkling his nose in distaste. 'A shameful way to treat a woman.'

In the end, through sheer force of character, Sarah won and her story was immortalized in a ballad called 'The Victory of Sarah'. She lived to an old age and her wishes regarding her daughters were fulfilled. One married into Parul, one into Chennamangalam. But the scandal took years to die down. Despite being cut off by her community, she brought up her daughters and educated them well and one of her grand-daughters became one of the first Malabari Jews to get a university degree.

Yet the people of both villages saw Sarah's story as shameful. They believed her liberal attitude set a bad example to the younger relatives. As we left his uncle's house at sun-down, it was clear Anil had some sympathy with Sarah's male relatives. She had been a handful and they were only doing their duty to protect her and the children.

'Even some modern girls can be like this,' he told me gravely. 'A big headache. It's not something I want. I don't want any trouble when I get married.'

'Do you think a bride from Israel would find it difficult to adjust?'

'A Kerala Jewish girl would be the best for me. But there are no Kerala Jewish girls. I have to find a wife from outside Kerala who wants to come here. But it's not easy. A person used to Indian culture finds western culture difficult to accept. Some people see us as primitive, but it's not that. This life is just a village life, no tension. For me it's the ultimate. When I

look around, nowhere is more beautiful than this. I'm very happy living here. I never had any racial discrimination, I have a lot of Muslim, Hindu, Christian friends. They tell me, "Why go to Israel?" But I need a wife.'

'She couldn't come here?'

'Everything changes. The whole lifestyle changes. I was born and brought up in Israel as a boy – I know the lifestyle and tastes there. Then I came to India, so for me, it's not difficult to adjust. For them, it's difficult. If you're jumping down the ladder, it's different. I cannot ask an Israeli girl to give up her western life for the village. I would have to be very lucky to find a girl such as this.'

'But many Israelis love India.'

'Loving India and living in India is different.'

We were now driving through a stretch of waterways that led directly towards the sea. Black clouds tumbled like boulders across the horizon, swiftly blotting out the last vestiges of light. The biggest storm for months was descending. We could hear the low roll of thunder from just across the hillside and in just a few minutes the whole sky would turn white with sheet and forked lightning. Anil already knew he had to leave. The choice was not really between Kerala and marriage. He could always marry a non-Jewish girl here and stay. The choice was more fundamental: between Kerala and his Jewishness. He had to lose one part of himself.

'This place, always, it absorbs you,' said Anil. 'But either I choose a bride who is not Jewish, or I leave Kerala for ever. That's the saddest part of all. You can't gain without com-

promise. If you want to live in Kerala, you have to compromise on the Jewishness. If you're not willing to compromise on the Jewishness, you cannot live in Kerala. That's the choice we face.'

'They should be queuing to come,' I told him as we bumped along the road home. In this unremitting onslaught of rain, the panorama that enveloped us was dramatic, primal, eternal. The storm had knocked out the electricity, plunging every house, every business, every road into darkness, turning sky, mountain and sea into a single entity of black. For a split second, the crackle of lightning illuminated the palm-fringed horizon that stretched before us. Then it was gone again. Anil knew what he was about to lose.

'They should be queuing, it's true,' Anil replied, struggling to see the road ahead as it became engulfed in rainwater that ran like quicksilver streams. 'But in order to win, we have to find the exceptions in life. The Jewish girl who will sacrifice everything for Kerala. But we can't always find the exceptions. If I want to live this Jewish life, I must leave everything I love. For Israel.'

Eleven

Roses in the Desert

'The sparrow has found his home at last,
The swallow, a nest for its young.'

Psalm, 84:3

Dawn was close at hand and the nightly solitude of the Negev would be broken soon as the sun emerged from behind the mountains. For now, the trunk road that snaked through the desert was desolate, but in less than an hour there would be juddering convoys heading for the ports, army trucks moving towards military checkpoints in the south, and carloads of commuters shuttling between Jerusalem and Tel Aviv. As the clouds of night dissipated like djinns shrinking away to their daytime lairs, the skies softened to a translucent grey and an immeasurable serenity emanated from the barren plains. When the sun finally surfaced, blinking into the new day, the grey skyline was streaked with stripes of candy pink. Set ablaze by the light, the desert came alive.

The plains reached across an expanse of terrain from the

Dead Sea down towards the blue finger of the Indian Ocean that pointed to Israel's southernmost tip, Eilat. Flanked to the east by mountains bordering Jordan and to the west by Egypt and the Palestinian territory of Gaza, this was pioneer country. When the first *moshavs* came here in the early fifties, they were equipped with little more than a determination to succeed, and from the sands they have summoned up whole communities.

By their very existence here they believed they were defending their country's borders, bringing a Jewish presence after centuries of exile. Some of the *moshavs* were within striking distance of the rocket launchers in Gaza. The ceaseless fear of attack, of being supplanted from this land, was coupled with the challenge of inducing the desert to bear life and hope. Yet many, including the Cochini Jews, welcomed the chance to settle here, even more than in the holy city of Jerusalem, for the desert held an older and equally sacred significance for them.

Abraham, the patriarch of the Jewish people known as 'father of the multitude', was inextricably linked with the Negev and specifically to the ancient city of Be'er Sheva, the capital of the region. The meaning of Be'er Sheva was 'well of the swearing', which referred to a past agreement between Abraham and a local ruler, Abimelech, whereby the prophet gained rights to use a well to water his flock.

By emulating the life of the prophet, settling here was imbued with religious significance. The sacrifice went beyond the merely physical and was a living metaphor for the Jewish

struggle. In the past the desert was seen as a place of death and chaos, depicted in the Bible as a 'howling wilderness', a 'land unsown', which appeared to have been abandoned by all things good. It was a visceral reminder of the despair endured by the ancient Jews during their forty-year sojourn in the desert before they were led to the Promised Land.

There was a moment after 1948 when the Cochini Jews feared they would not be allowed to make the *aliyah* after all. Before being granted permission to resettle, the Cochinis were visited by an official from the Jewish Agency on behalf of the nascent state. In his report, he voiced grave concerns about the suitability of this people to settle in Israel. In particular, he was worried about their small stature, weak constitution and the prevalence of elephantiasis, fearing this would spread to the motherland. The *Report on the Jews of Malabar* described them as small, weak and thin, with many suffering from 'a disease transmitted via mosquito larvae deposited on the skin at night and which burrow in through the moisture from the sleeper's perspiration'. It added: 'More than fifty per cent of all Jewish families... subsist... under acute want... the majority live on rice and fish... malnutrition is widespread.' An Israeli physician recommended that the Cochinis were resettled in very dry regions, with great variations in temperature, which would minimize the risk of the condition spreading. For this reason, many ended up in the Negev.

In a later report in 1949, the official said he feared the Cochinis were unrealistic about the tough conditions they would face. He warned that they would have to work very

hard as farmers in Israel. But the idealism of the Jews of Kerala could not be dampened. All they could focus on was finally going home.

On arrival, it proved to be every bit as tough as the Israeli officials had forewarned. In particular, the Cochinis found it difficult to adjust to living in a country that constantly had to be braced for battle. In 1973 Gilbert Kushner wrote *Immigrants from India in Israel*, in which he describes a night patrol with a Cochini guard on his round at 2 a.m.:

> Aaron, one of the Cochini on guard duty tonight, is especially concerned about not tripping in the darkness for he is carrying a loaded rifle and wearing a heavy cartridge belt. He holds the weapon clumsily as if it were a piece of wood. I ask him to make sure the safety lever is on... On the way back up the hill, Aaron tells me this never happened in Cochin...

The vast majority of Cochini Jews settled in *moshavs* across the south of Israel. Several settlements were almost exclusively theirs. These were complete townships with their own residential district, shops and even a synagogue, all a short drive away from Be'er Sheva. Sixty years on, these communities were thriving, thanks to new marriages and births. In one *moshav* in the south of the Negev, the Cochinis had recreated their old land, calling it Little Kerala. The fear of demise that afflicted the people in India no longer tormented those resettled in Israel. The *aliyah* had facilitated a rebirth for the Jews of Kerala.

The transition from India to Israel was all the more remarkable given that they had not come from, say, the Rajasthan desert, but had traded a land blessed with fertility for the barrenness of the Negev. Many of the Cochinis had rarely ventured beyond southern India, so they had never known the true desert, only the biblical depictions of suffering followed by deliverance. Their excitement on arriving in the land of Abraham was accompanied by an initial sense of dislocation. It was the opposite of everything they had ever known: in Kerala, water, trees, flowers, life itself are taken for granted. Into the cracked and hardened landscape of the Negev, they had to discover ways of instilling some of the vibrancy, fertility and life of their old home.

There, they had had every natural advantage. Throw a seed to the ground, leave it untouched, unnourished by human hand and it will flourish and proliferate. In Kerala they luxuriated in an abundance of water and its gifts, whether it was the Arabian Sea, the lotus-strewn lakes or backwaters shaded by tendrils of tropical flowers. If they wanted milk, there were buffalos that ambled like stately memsahibs in the surrounding fields. If they wanted fruits and vegetables, they only need step into their gardens. In Israel, the Jews of Cochin were tested. It proved to be the making of some of them.

A month or so after visiting Kerala, I was driving to Shahar to meet one such man. Eliahu Bezalel had come to Israel in the very first wave of Cochini immigration in the early 1950s. In India he had been, by his own admission, a young man of little consequence but with large ambitions. He

had just a few rupees in his pocket when he embarked on the *aliyah*. On arrival his first job seemed to hold little promise of achievement or greatness. He was a shepherd, but he carried out his duties with diligence and pride, for even the smallest task was part of the wider effort to build Israel. This was the homecoming the Jews had prayed for in Kerala for two thousand years: 'Next year, in Jerusalem,' they toasted one another at each festival.

Shahar was more than an hour and a half from Jerusalem on the road to Be'er Sheva, past the turning towards Gaza. After interminable vistas of reds and browns, breathing in air as acrid as the ochre dust that enveloped the horizon, I saw the landscape melt into a shimmer of softest green. As my Palestinian taxi driver, Nazeeh, drove into the heart of the settlement, all around we could see long, white, tent-like nurseries that sheltered fragile seedlings. The trees, shrubs and lawns were verdant, with the vividness of a freshly watered springtime. The settlement was made up of suburban avenues of whitewashed bungalows in neat rows with well-groomed gardens, some complete with white picket fences and lawns nourished by sprinkler systems that could put the proudest English country gardener to shame. Framing the roadside were bushes of billowing roses and fig trees, fragrant with ripe fruit. In this suburban utopia, one could almost forget this was a desert of the East until one's gaze was drawn to the middle horizon beyond the white fences. There lay the realities that the inhabitants kept at bay every day, relentless desert dunes and the blur of low mountain ridges that signalled

the Jordanian border. Away from the *moshav* dream, underlying every Jew's romantic ambition to make the desert of the Holy Land bloom, there was the unceasing nature of the struggle to conserve life in these lands and the vulnerability of its tightly drawn borders.

Nazeeh was surprised as he slowly drove past the pretty houses, with children playing outside, their chocolate-drop eyes, glossy dark skin and black kinked hair all signalling that we were in the right place. With its palms, bougainvillea and tropical flowers, this could still be India. The Cochinis had created a corner of Kerala in the Israeli desert, even copying the village-style bungalows with red-tiled roofs and airy pillared porches. Pink blossom trailed over low walls. Flocks of sparrows chirruped among the date palms, periodically taking off to skim the skies in tight triangular formations like Israeli Air Defence squadrons on patrol.

The house of Bezalel was one of the prettiest, with the best-kept garden, as if it belonged in a postcard. A young man who looked like a Cochin Jew squatted among the flower beds, his forearms a burnished copper, wrenching out stubborn weeds. His skin glistened with sweat as the white disc of the sun burned overhead. His face was shaded by a wide-brimmed straw hat. Seeing strangers, he paused from digging, looked up and smiled, his teeth bright and dazzling, before turning back to the flowerbeds. I was to learn that this was Bezalel's young son, who lived next door and was taking over the running of the family's horticultural business.

The old man himself was inside in the kitchen that

overlooked the rear garden. He was recovering from a recent operation on his knee a few weeks ago. It had left him housebound and only able to walk with the aid of a walking frame. Bezalel was in his late seventies but retained a touch of the rakish good looks that were evident in the photographs that lined the walls of his house, where as a young man in a black suit and skinny tie he posed jauntily with Israeli leaders shortly after his arrival. There were also modern-day portraits of him receiving awards and medals from the President of India or Prime Minister of Israel for services to horticulture or Indo-Israeli relations.

From being a poor young émigré from India who arrived with just 250 rupees in his pocket, he had become an ambassador for the Indian Jewish community, an emblem of the success that can come from hard work and devotion. Stepping into his home, I could smell the pungent tang of curry powder in the air: cumin, coriander, black pepper – the smells of Cochin's tropical marketplace that first enticed the merchant seamen of King Solomon to India's shores almost three millennia ago.

Bezalel's wife and daughter, older and younger versions of the same woman, were bustling around the kitchen, laying out the requisite snacks and drinks of iced lemonade with chopped fresh mint before heading off to their lunchtime appointments. Bezalel sat with me at the table, now spread with homemade cakes, pastries and deliciously tart sliced apple from the Golan Heights. His face was worn with pain and as he rested his hands on the kitchen table, I noticed his

fingernails were blackened from recent treatment for prostate cancer, something he barely mentioned.

For despite illness, the physical discomfort and pain he bore, one sensed Bezalel was a man fulfilled, whose young man's ambition had been sated. First he had made the journey from India to Israel. Then he had risen from ordinary shepherd, to soldier, to businessman to ambassador not just for his new country, but for Kerala. From this tiny agricultural community in the Negev, as small and unremarkable as any Indian village, Bezalel had accomplished much and reached beyond his narrow world into one where he consorted with leaders and delivered lectures on his business and Indo-Jewish culture to audiences from Jerusalem to Delhi to Washington.

The source of all this was a simple idea. Bezalel had won his fame by making the wastelands of the Negev bloom. He had brought roses to the desert, and helped turn it into one of the biggest exports of the Israeli economy. Now in his late seventies, he could contemplate a legacy that went beyond mere commerce. He was married to a Cochini Jewess called Batzion and they had four children: two sons and two daughters. Last, but most important of all, he was a grandfather. He took none of this for granted, especially when he heard of how things had worked out in his old country. But when he left in the fifties, such things were not on the mind of a young man looking for adventure.

Every Jew who came to Israel harboured different motives. Bezalel left his village of Chennamangalam, the village that was home to four great religions, with the aim of living the

Zionist dream. He fervently believed in Zionism, which the Cochini Jews had grown up with even before the horrors of the Second World War. They lived in a place where the Jews had never been persecuted. They never encountered the cold fear that so many of their brethren experienced elsewhere. They had lived alongside Hindu, Muslim and Christian for millennia in India, free to be Jewish as well as Indian. And yet the Zionist dream lived on in the hearts of men like Bezalel. It harked back to the days when the Second Temple was broken and the Jews were driven out. They never forgot that Cochin, or 'Little Jerusalem' as they sometimes called it, was only a facsimile of that past life.

Cecil Koder, one of the old Cochini residents, wrote a poem in the 1930s which summed up their feelings:

It is our sincere ambition,
To be freed from foreign domination.
Palestine is our inspiration,
To build our home, a Jewish nation.

For God is always on our side,
He is our sincere guide,
Then why should we fear,
When we have Him near,
In days of sorrow and darkness.

We have passed through darker situation,
And won for us thrilling admiration,
Jerusalem is our destination.
The home and hope of our salvation.

Now we make an open declaration
To every anti-Jewish nation,
All their baseless, ruthless persecution
Will never bring our ruination.

The words seem grimly prophetic of what was to come in
Europe. What struck me about the poem was the sense of un-
wavering determination. For men like Koder and Bezalel,
Zionism was not born of their experiences in India; it was a
matter of righting the wrongs of a broader history. 'It was
pure Zionism,' Bezalel said as he explained his motivation to
come here, 'to build the country.'

At the start of the 1940s there were around two thousand
Jews in Cochin. After the formation of the state of Israel in
1948, the migration began in earnest in 1950 and within a
few decades there were less than fifty Jews left in Kerala. The
primary reason to go was to return to the land of their forefathers. But they were also driven to leave by poor economic
prospects. Their economic decline began once the British
Empire made the port cities of Bombay and Calcutta central
to their trading business, reducing Cochin's importance. With
Indian independence in 1947 the old system of colonial rule
and princely states bestowing privileges on favourites became
a thing of the past. Kerala was now part of the new secular
India and the special privileges that had been enjoyed by the
Jews from the time of Joseph Rabban were abolished.

The Cochini Jews lost out on trade, then the nascent
Indian government further impeded their business with a ban

on imports of luxury goods. Kerala's Communist state government also nationalized key industries and businesses, such as the ferry service, which had been a profitable Jewish-owned concern. In 1957 private land estates, including those of the old Jewish land barons, were seized, nationalized and redistributed among the population. This was followed in 1979 by the nationalization of the Jewish-run electric company.

The old certainties were gone for ever. The young looked around them in India and saw that the economic and political privileges that had taken centuries to build were now stripped away. Not that the Jews were specifically targeted in any way; it was all part of a wider political dynamic.

Then there was the issue of marriage. Intermarriage between Black and White Jews was still taboo in the 1950s. This reduced the choice of marriage partners for the young and the pressure to conform to the way of the elders was suffocating. Whenever the Black and White Jews came together, their past joined them like a difficult and unwanted guest at the dinner table.

The prospect of a new country, a Jewish homeland which needed people to build its infrastructure, industry, communities from scratch, was appealing to many of the Cochini Jews, particularly those with little money, land or prospects in India. Israel also represented a new beginning in another key way. It was a country for all Jews, regardless of colour or ethnicity. The Black Jews, in particular, saw a chance for a future unencumbered by the prejudices of the past. For all these reasons – Zionism, faith, economics, marriage and freedom – many Jews decided to quit Kerala for ever.

Some of the old guard feared the 'new exodus', as they termed it, was evidence of the old curse on the Kerala Jews. Those left behind lamented that their past sins were being paid for as they watched loved ones pack up and go. The answer to this fatalism may be to look at what happened to the Cochini Jews once they settled in Israel.

It proved to be a renaissance of sorts. Today, there are 5,000 Jews in Israel with Cochini blood. They are spread all over the country, from the northernmost border with Lebanon to *moshavs* deep in the Negev, as well as pockets of communities in Haifa and Jerusalem. As Bezalel told me, this blossoming of the Kerala Jews in Israel sprang from the dust beneath their feet when families like his arrived in the 1950s.

*

'It was totally barren, there was nothing,' said Bezalel, gently grazing his grey stubble with black fingernails. 'We lived in a small wooden building with 26 square metres for each family. That was the only thing. In three years we built the first proper house with the help of the Jewish Agency. And in 1958 I married Batzion in this village. She's from the Mattancheri community,' he told me.

Such were the foundations of a new life. In the first years of marriage, the couple purchased land and experimented with a new agricultural business. At the time there were sixty families in the *moshav*, most of whom were North African

Jews. Gradually, more Cochini families came to settle here and the two communities bonded.

'They didn't know where we came from. They didn't know of India's ancient culture or its history of Jews, so at first they kept their distance. After some years we settled and it came to the point where we, the Cochinis, were the first to lead the whole village towards development.'

Bezalel proved to be a natural leader and businessman. He started by growing flowers for export. It was a new venture and would have been risky even in the most benevolent of climates. In the midst of the desert, in a country fighting for its very survival, it seemed a hopeless enterprise. He began with gladioli. By the sixties, Bezalel had achieved the feat of selling flowers to Holland and won first prize for exporting gladioli from the Israeli Prime Minister. The central government spotted the wider potential and in 1966 approached him to develop a modern greenhouse industry in the Negev.

'Naturally, I agreed. I went to study greenhouse techniques in London and Holland. When I came back we started the first modern, climate-controlled greenhouse in this village. The first in the country,' he told me. His eyes sparkled as he recollected the experiment. By growing his gladioli and then selling them overseas, he was playing his part in the Zionist dream of establishing a viable country, with its own industries, pioneering technologies and innovation. Soon, his ambitions moved up a gear. He was ready to move from gladioli to roses.

'It took five years. Then I decided this was a nice area for

growing roses for export. At first I met with scepticism. It was several years before people understood this was a profitable business and then they started to copy.'

The horticultural export business developed from these modest beginnings. Neighbouring *moshavs* observed the Shahar experiment and followed suit. Bezalel was exporting roses and gladioli to Holland and met increasing demand by building vast greenhouses that ringed the settlement. By this stage the government and export ministry were lending their help and finance to develop the infrastructure to get the industry off the ground. 'Within ten to fifteen years Israel became the third largest exporter of flowers to Holland. I was part of that effort,' Bezalel explained simply.

Indeed, flowers became one of the biggest agricultural exports for Israel. The trade that began in Bezalel's back yard escalated to a scale he had never imagined. But decades later his work was partly undone by a combination of technological advance, hyper-inflation and the war with Lebanon which broke out in 1984.

The war's effect was crippling. Conflict with neighbours was an alien concept for the Kerala Jews, who had enjoyed peaceful relations for millennia in India with all faiths, including Muslims, apart from very brief periods in history when they came under attack from the Moors and Portuguese.

Inflation rocketed out of control in Israel and the economy was hit hard. People defaulted on loans and as war raged on its northern border, the government struggled to stabilize an economy that was in freefall.

'Many businesses collapsed, many went bankrupt, many committed suicide,' Bezalel recalled flatly. Things then improved after a few years as stability returned and exports picked up a little. But by the 1990s, his business faced a new enemy: globalization. Israel's flower growers were priced out of the market by new, cheaper producers from Third World countries such as Kenya and Zimbabwe, where the cost of production was a fraction of Israel's.

'We pay $26 a day for a worker and in Africa it is $1 a day. We have very big payments for water, electricity, for heating or cooling the greenhouses. In Africa they don't have these costs. So they reduced the price. The market price has therefore gone down so much we can't compete. Now everywhere in the Negev you are seeing empty greenhouses; this is the reason.' I had seen the redundant greenhouse tents myself, their billowing, white canopies flapping in the red dust winds.

I asked him what he was doing now. Bezalel still grew his roses on one and a quarter acres but said this summer that too would end. His new business was grapes, as well as ginger and tapioca – staples of his native Kerala. 'The Brazilians are dying for that. Maybe next year we'll try new crops.'

Bezalel was a survivor and therefore suited to this life. He and his family had all adjusted well to the Israeli way. Of his children one had married a Jewish Canadian, one a Bulgarian, and another daughter married a South African. They lived nearby and she ran a Cochini catering business in one of the disused greenhouses, catering to Israelis and tourists who

wanted to taste Kerala cuisine. Her business was successful
and a link to their old heritage.

His family had never had a problem integrating, unlike
other Kerala Jews who came here. Bezalel never felt uncomfortable in Israel like some of his old countrymen such as
Babu, who had been driven to tears when thinking of his
experience here.

'What was it like when you first came to Israel?' I asked
him. 'You came from a country where the Jews had lived for
more than two thousand years with no persecution and total
security. Here the situation is so different.' The Kerala Jews
had gone from a life of peace to one of almost perpetual
insecurity and conflict, a struggle for survival in their yearned-
for haven; where once Muslims had been friends, now they
were potential enemies of the state. It was deeply disturbing,
this constant 'suspicion of the stranger, the dark face' as Babu
had put it.

Bezalel nodded avidly in agreement. He had always had
happy relations with the Muslims during his life in Kerala.
After all, Chennamangalam was a city which represented
religious harmony. Yet he had left behind the life of that
village and Kerala and here he fervently believed that his
primary duty was to protect his new country from potential
enemies. In India the Muslims had been friends, in Israel it
was necessary to defend oneself. Bezalel was an unapologetic
realist.

It was a massive mental adjustment, yet he had readily
made the sacrifice, jettisoning the old ways. In India he had

been a simple villager, a man of peace. In Israel he had fought in two wars for his new country, in 1967 and then in 1973. Every chance to prove oneself was relished, even though he had no prior knowledge or experience of conflict. A fervent Zionist, he chose to push himself to the limit, to do more, not less; to take on the riskiest of enterprises. As a soldier, he had no compunction about tackling Muslim soldiers from Israel's border enemies. His was the pragmatism of a natural warrior, whether in business or in battle.

'When we were first training in the army I was asked which group I wanted to join. I chose mine clearance,' he said in a quiet, determined voice, stripped of conceit or emotion, relaying the bare facts. 'Our officer said to us, "You're the only people who'll never make a second mistake." I liked that. I served almost fourteen years. Now my children have all been officers in the army. This is part of the life of Israel.'

For him war became his normality and it forged bonds with his fellow Israelis in a way that could never be broken. He learned the nature of Israel during his service. 'When you're serving your time, in that group you have a bank manager, a professor, a doctor, a road-sweeping man. Everybody together. We eat together, we sleep together, living as one for those days. All backgrounds, all colours, all different types of Jew. Everybody knew we had no second choice, we must fight for our survival. That doesn't just mean fight with gun, it means fight to be the best at business, the best at sport, to struggle for the nation. Otherwise we can't survive. Everybody felt we had to come together. We had a feeling: it

doesn't matter if we work ten, twelve, fourteen hours a day. It doesn't matter because we're building.'

He helped build his nation in many guises: shepherd, soldier, forester and road maintenance man. But his big idea, his real contribution was not in war but in helping to build the peace. 'Once we had success, many people came to visit us here. The first were two famous French philosophers. What was the name? They came to study us, to find out if there was any problem with colour and Indians in Israel. But there was no racism, nothing *I* felt.'

Yet he mentioned that sometimes his children were teased at school because of their dark colouring. He took it in his stride. 'When they went to school, one time my second son was crying because all the other children called him Nigger or negro or black, black, black. Then we told him *why* we are black. That way they understood. Then later, all the important personalities, ministers, even Prime Ministers, came here to see our farm because we took the lead in that.'

In 1994 he received the highest accolade of all. Prime Minister Yitzhak Rabin awarded Bezalel the Kaplan prize for his work in agriculture. The Indian ambassador hosted a party in his honour and told Bezalel his work had given Indians in Israel a good name. But a further honour was to come. At the end of 2005, as Bezalel was receiving radiation treatment for his prostate cancer, he received a call from the Indian ambassador.

'Three days before finishing my radiation, I was travelling every day to the hospital in Jerusalem and then coming home.

At this time, the ambassador called me and said, "Stop the car and talk with me." I said, "What happened?" He said, "No, no, no. You've been awarded the Pravasi Bharti Diwas award and you must fly in five days to Hyderabad to get the award from the President of India in January."

'When I returned, I went to my professor who was treating me and I told him I had to fly. He said, "On the last day, come early and at eight o'clock we will give you radiation, then come back at four o'clock and we'll give second radiation." The next day he checked me and said I could fly. I went with my wife to the function.'

He showed me the award, which was framed and hung on his wall of memories. It was signed by President Abdul Kalam, India's Muslim head of state, and bore the crest of three lions. He stroked the crest with his forefinger very gently.

'I was chosen from Indians all over the world. Eleven of us were chosen for this. Two thousand Indians came from all over the world for the function. The others awarded were very big businessmen, from places like the United States. I felt like a fly between these elephants.'

I asked if he felt it had been his destiny to come to Israel to achieve all this, that his life might not have been so enriched had he stayed in Cochin. He laughed. 'Oh, I don't know.' Then he thought a bit and added, 'See, I think I had a nice circle of life. That means I started something which brought good things for Israel, good things for India. Now maybe in my next trip to Kerala, to Chennamangalam, I'll try to find people to develop tourism in my village. Because Chennamangalam has

a speciality. In 1987 I was invited to Washington by the North American Jewish Flower Growers Association. There I had to give a lecture about my life in India and then in Israel. Then I explained about Chennamangalam.

'Chennamangalam is the only place, maybe in the world, where four religions stay together. That means Jew, Muslim, Hindu and Christian. Each has its specialty. The Hindu worshippers blow the conch shell on festivals, the Muslims call "*Allahu Akhbar*", the Jews call with *shofar* and the Christians with bell. Once every seven or eight years, the festivals come at the same time and when this time comes, you can hear them together: you can hear the conch shell, you can hear the bell, you can hear the *shofar* and the call of the mosque. Everything. This happens only in Chennamangalam. There is nowhere else in the world. Not even in Jerusalem, which has only three.'

The new ambition of the old man who brought roses to Israel's desert landscape was to disseminate that message of religious unity, a message that Kerala had instilled in him, to a wider audience.

'Do you miss Kerala ever?'

'No, truly.' He lightly touched his heart, then took a slice of Golan apple and bit into it as he considered his choice. 'Kerala is nice to travel and enjoy. But not for living. Because there's no adventurous life there. Here, every day we have the challenge. Every day we have fighting, struggle, murder, problems. That makes a big difference. Kerala is a calm, cool, quiet place. Israel is our struggle for survival.'

*

Bezalel was one example of a Cochini Jew who had made
Israel work for his family. There were others. After Shahar I
went to a place called 'Little India' to meet Isaac Chaim
Nehemia, who was one of the most senior Cochini Jewish
elders and a leader of the Indian Jews in Israel. He lived in
Nevatim, the biggest Cochini settlement in the area which lay
southeast of Be-er Sheva. Here, 120 Cochini families and 600
people had settled.

Nevatim was, perhaps, the most developed of the *moshavs*
where the Cochinis had settled. It had its own Kerala-style
synagogue, a museum about the old history and it observed
the faith in the traditional Indian Jewish manner. In terms of
sheer numbers, it was very successful, although less prosperous
than its small neighbour Shahar. As we drove into the *moshav*,
the temperature was beginning to drop. In a few hours, the
chill of desert evening skies would be with us. Nevatim had
none of the regulated perfection of Shahar: the houses looked
less fancy and more run down, the gardens and communal
areas were not as green and pristine, with lawns overgrown
and slightly brown. All around us the red desert plains closed
in, like a sleeping sea, with the mountain ranges of Jordan
beyond.

Disused greenhouses lay abandoned here and there. Like
Shahar, Nevatim had suffered a collapse in its flower export
business due to competition from African farmers. So many
of its residents now worked in Be'er Sheva in regular day jobs,

abandoning the land that has begun to revert to its natural state.

But Nevatim remained a clean and friendly neighbour-hood. Cochini Jews walked their dogs, children played on the streets safely and everyone seemed happy to help a stranger. Old women tended their gardens or sat in wicker chairs watching the desert skyline change colour. A middle-aged matron speed-walked down the main road, ample, ghee-upholstered buttocks jostling inside tight sweatpants. Some of the older generation adopted a fusion Indian-Israeli frontier-style of dressing – one lady wore her silky salwar kameez under a zipped-up fleece jacket, while another old man lounged in his garden in a woolly jumper pulled over the lungi, supplemented with woolly socks and Nike trainers. The local children were unmistakably Cochini. One girl aged about eight stopped skipping with her friends and turned slowly to watch our car as we parked to find our bearings. A curtain of dark curly hair fell over one eye as she looked over her shoulder to scrutinize us; her skin was glossy, almost as black as the teak of Kerala, and her eyes the colour of molasses.

Youngsters like the girl still celebrated the Jewish festivals the Kerala way, they ate Cochini food, they retained unmis-takable south Indian features, and yet most had never seen India. Hebrew not Malayalam is spoken here and the young are marrying non-Cochini and even non-Indian Jews. It is accepted that Cochini-only marriages are becoming a thing of the past, even in Nevatim. Slowly, the old Cochin life was

being diluted, absorbed into the pan-Israeli national identity that is needed in order to keep the state strong.

Yet I was impressed it had lasted thus far. After fifty years, Cochin remains very much alive in Israel. I was to meet a man who had already succeeded in building the first Cochini synagogue in Israel, the first Cochini museum. Now he wanted to turn Nevatim into a tourist destination for the south, branding it as 'Little India'. His daughter Nili, a feisty young woman who took tours of the museum, helped her mother Miriam run a Jewish-Indian catering business. All of them showed that the Cochini dream was not dying, merely evolving.

I turned up at Isaac Nehemia's house mid-afternoon. His house was one of the biggest in the *moshav*: simple, modern and whitewashed, with an adjoining garage large enough for a fleet of cars. Inside, it was full of homely touches and clean lines: white stone floors, white walls and blinds at the windows. All the other rooms led off a large central living area, with a dining room and seating area with plump leather sofas and a massive television. The kitchen led off towards the back of the house, exuding enticing smells of curry and chutneys.

Isaac was a wonderful character, a blend of the Israeli and Indian Jew: loud, gregarious, irrepressible and captivating. He wore a casual brown shirt, with rolled-up sleeves and open neck. On his bald head he wore a skullcap made of cotton fabric printed with bright tropical palm leaves, as if in tribute to his old motherland. His eyes shone with child-like delight

and when he spoke in his booming baritone it was like listening to a roaring river. His conversation would twist and turn with boundless energy, catching you in its momentum and carrying you along, leaving you happily exhausted by the ride. At the end of a particularly satisfying anecdote, he would throw his head back and laugh with delight, slamming the table with the edge of his fist. There was no reserve or artful modesty with this man. He had the brash directness of the Israelis softened by an Indian's emotional warmth. Like his daughter, his smile was enchanting. What God had taken away from Isaac in the hair department, He made up for by way of teeth. Isaac's smile was a joy to behold.

The two were very close and the father evidently loved teasing his daughter. She in turn adored his stories, even though she had clearly heard them so many times before. Very quickly, I felt as if I'd known these two for ever. Nili was born in Israel with her five brothers. Her parents had come when they were still children. Nevatim started off as a small Jewish settlement in 1946, before the formation of Israel. Isaac and his family came in 1954.

The Negev had once been populated by Arabs and particularly the Bedouins. Nomadic tribes living in the desert dated back to the time of the Prophet Abraham himself. Today the Bedouins still have a market which takes place every Thursday in the southern part of Be'er Sheva, where they trade camels, sheep and goats. Yet it has become more of a show for the tourists, with some of the tribe selling crafts to earn extra income.

Given the Bedouin tradition in the desert, many Jewish families who settled here believed they were safeguarding the land for their own people, said Nili. 'The Jewish population in the Negev was isolated and it was mostly Arab around here, so they wanted to protect this area which is where Israel would be. There were eleven settlements like this, one was *moshav* Nevatim, but we the Jewish of Cochin only came in 1954.'

They followed another group of Jews who had failed to settle here successfully. They did not know who these people were, merely that the life in the desert had not suited them. The Cochinis were the next group of immigrants to take up the challenge of desert life. Isaac was just thirteen when he arrived with his parents. Like Bezalel, he remembered it as a bleak place.

'There was nothing, no plants, just dry, dry land. I looked at the desert and cried. I told my mother, "Why you come here? Why we leave Kerala? Kerala is a very beautiful place."' He re-enacted the scene of Isaac the boy, full of tears and horror at the new homeland, weeping and tugging his mother's arm.

'But, my mother said: "Son, listen. This is the place Abraham started and built the presence in Israel long ago. Great history is here. Be'er Sheva is the start for the Jewish people. If we start working, this place will be our paradise."'

His mother was the dominant force in the family and very religious. His grandfather, Abraham Nehemia, had been one of the elders in the Thekumbhagam Synagogue in Ernakulam.

They had decided to come after a man from the Jewish Agency visited Cochin in 1949 to talk to the community about Israel. 'He told us, "Israel is now independent, we want Israelis from all over the world to come, Cochin Jews please come." We said yes.' He guffawed with laughter. 'Yeees, we said, because this is our Israel.'

His mother called the shots in their household. When he asked her why she had wanted to come here, she told the young boy they came to build a homeland. 'She said, "We will work the land and if we work the land it'll give us everything." Our Torah said Israel is the land of milk and honey. We believed our country would provide for us. Everything we grow here will be successful.'

At first it was not so. The first effort to grow crops failed. The *moshav* had seventy-two families then and they seemed set to fail. Then some of the younger generation took specialist agricultural studies, including Isaac. After leaving the army, he returned to form a plan to make the *moshav* work. The plan involved planting vegetables and fruit and rearing chickens. Not everyone could make it work. It was tough and around fifty per cent of the original settlers abandoned it for the north.

It was 1961 when Isaac began to put his plan into action. The community planted fruit trees such as apricots and peaches. 'These fruits need cool weather but in the spring time, when it makes the fruit, it needs hot weather during day and coolness at night time. I said, this tree you must plant here. It was success. Yeeah!

'When we started, this was the weakest *moshav* and within a few years it was one of the most successful economically.' From fruit trees, they went into flowers like Shahar and soon Nevatim was also exporting to Europe and earning a good income. In 1964, Isaac married a Cochini Jew who was born in Bombay. Miriam and Isaac had six children.

The *moshav* grew until it was the biggest Cochini settlement in Israel. Then the 1984 war hit and like many others, the *moshav*'s business slumped. Isaac knew everything had changed. 'I told the people of Nevatim, it's finished.'

But he was not beaten yet. He had another plan and this one entailed drawing upon the Kerala history. 'My community has a big history, a great history. I want to make a reminder of it here,' he told me. He was in his late sixties and it would be his last big project, a legacy of sorts. He began some years ago by taking an architect from Israel to Cochin to see the synagogues there. Then a replica was built in his community.

Miriam and her daughter also did their part by running a kitchen which catered to Israelis and foreigners. Earlier that day they had given thirty tourists a breakfast of *idli* and *sambar*. Miriam brought out leftovers for us to try. Tourism was to be Nevatim's future. Already Isaac was marking out a vision which comprised new roads, water pumps, enhanced sewage systems, to prepare for the coming of the tourists. He wanted to build an Indian Culture theatre and host conferences and meetings here. It sounded like a costly investment and where would the money come from? But Isaac was

undeterred by the practicalities. He had his vision and it would become real.

'I see a small Kerala here. We want to show people our canals, the water, the fishnets of Cochin,' he told me as his great hands conjured visions of the future, mapped upon his kitchen table. His Tropicana *kippah* had slipped down in his excitement and he readjusted it.

I asked how his people had settled here among other Israelis and he explained that many were now marrying non-Indian Jews. There was a better understanding of the great depth of history and culture of their people. This instilled a natural sense of self-worth, said Nili. 'I can say in Israel, the Cochin Jewry were successful in immigration. We don't suffer from feeling we're lower than other Israelis.'

Yet it was evident that colour continued to be an issue at times in Israel as well. Their neighbours, the Ethiopian Jews, felt it and drew comfort from the Cochinis, who seemed incredibly self-assured. The source of the Cochini Jews' self-assurance was, perhaps, their history.

'We left India as a very proud people and we're still a very proud people here,' Nili explained. 'Even the younger genera-tion who've entered mixed marriages, they say, I am Cochini. They're still proud. Nobody can say to me, "You are less than me." Some Ethiopian Israelis used to ask me: "How come you don't feel less in Israel, because you're dark?" I said to them, "First of all I have a beautiful colour. I am chocolate and everyone wants our colour, you know." Here, we have an Ashkenazim school, and they're all white. On friendly days

they say to us, "You have a beautiful colour." Then when they want to tease us, they say, "Oh, you are dark like chocolate." I say to them, "And you are cheese. Cheese is less tasty than chocolate."' She smiled at her story and glanced at her father for approval.

Then she added more seriously that sometimes the issue of colour evoked the old Cochini divide. 'One Ashkenazim said to me in the museum, "You're not Jewish because you're black." I said: "Abraham was a dark man was he not? Not blue eyed and blond." All of his friends told me I was right. And I told him, "Now you need to ask yourself who you are."'

However proud she was of her Jewish Indian culture and however bold she was in defending it, Nili acknowledged it would be difficult to preserve, as so many Kerala Jews were marrying outsiders within Israel. She remained optimistic for herself, all the same, telling me if she could not find a Cochini man to marry, then she would marry an outsider and instil in her husband the Kerala ways. I had no doubt of it, for behind her father's smile lay her grandmother's indomitable will.

'It's what I want. It's in my blood,' she said firmly, running her fingers through her bobbed hair. 'It's never going away, no matter who I marry. See, my aunty married an Ashkenazi. He told her, "Wife, I will never eat spice." Every Shabbat she would lovingly make her spiciest chicken dish from Cochin. Every Shabbat he would refuse. After so many refusals, on so many Shabbats, he now eats the same food. He even asks for this one dish. This will be my way also.'

*

It was night by the time I left Nevatim. The desert was cold and empty as we climbed into the car to leave the father and daughter on the threshold, waving their goodbyes. They had shown me their community, complete with a gaily painted replica of the Ernakulam Synagogue and the museum. After fifty years, the Cochini Jewish way of life was thriving in the Middle East just as it was dying in southern India. The community here took every opportunity to push things forward to the next generation. They were ruthless in their pragmatism, as one would expect of a desert people. If they could not marry a Cochini, then they would marry another Jew and show them the Kerala Jewish life. It was better than the alternative.

My thoughts settled on Nili and her good-humoured determination to make her future husband love Cochin as much as he loved her. She was very much the modern Israeli woman and yet, despite having never set foot in Cochin, she was unmistakably a daughter of Kerala. I remembered Anil Abraham's ardent wish as he played with the peppercorn necklace beside the riverbank near Parul. Here was one Jewish girl who would not give him headaches.

As Nazeeh and I drove away, heading back to Jerusalem, I considered these remarkable stories of adaptation. The elders had plucked whole communities from the tropics and transplanted them to the desert. The motivation of the people I had met so far had been Zionism, to follow in the footsteps

of Abraham and take on the toughest of assignments to bring a Jewish renewal to the Negev. The differences between what they sacrificed and what they embraced were marked not just by the contrasting landscapes, but equally in the religious mentality of the Jewish communities in India and Israel. Kerala offered a conservative, highly traditional and orthodox way of life for the Jews. Israel was the Jewish homeland and yet it was fast-paced, modern and secular. Even Isaac had noted the difference when he first arrived as a boy, telling me that he was shocked to see people working on Shabbat, to see that not every community had a synagogue as a right. In westernized secular Israel, the synagogue was not the absolute centre of life as it was in rural Kerala.

I was driving beneath a canopy of velvet blue skies on the road towards the Holy City that remained the heartbeat of the faith which sustained the Jewish people even in their long exile and dispersal. Always, day or night, when travelling through these lands, past signposts that were not mere traffic directions but markers of history, one was overwhelmed by the past. This was more true in Jerusalem than in any other place I had ever seen. In the morning I would meet a man who had come to Israel more than thirty years ago. Not for Zionism, for he was not a politically minded man, nor was he a man who sought economic opportunity or freedom from Kerala. Abraham Eliavoo had come to Israel for the love of his faith. He had come to immerse himself in the history of his people and to be part of the ultimate religious experience of living in the Holy City. Being a religious man, he had seen it

as his duty to leave behind the privilege and comfort of his village in India to end his life in the city of Solomon. He lived with his family here, he worked for the good of the nation and prayed regularly at the Western Wall, which still had the power to move him to tears even now. The dream had been realized. And yet all was not well in Jerusalem.

Twelve

Home

'So when God destroyed the cities of the plain, He remembered Abraham, and He brought Lot out of the catastrophe that overthrew the cities where Lot had lived.'

Genesis, 19:29

It was five o'clock in the morning and most of Jerusalem was sleeping. Abraham awoke for prayers. His body was stiff from cold and his bad leg always proved more resistant to movement at this time. He reached out for his stick and hauled himself on to his feet. After prayers, he ate breakfast and prepared to leave for work as an accountant at the Star of David emergency services organization in the centre of town. He had to be out of the house by 6.30 in order to catch the bus on time. His working day began at 7.30 through to three in the afternoon, six days a week. Afterwards, he would go to the local shopping mart and pick up some provisions before taking the bus home. After making his way up the steep pathway and steps, he finally reached the house and let himself

in. There, he would prepare a cup of tea, not proper Indian chai which was boiled in a pan with milk, sugar and black leaves, but the inadequate sort made with a bag dipped in hot water. Afterwards, he would make something to eat and await the family's return at night.

It would be a gruelling routine for a young man in his prime, but Abraham was seventy-eight and unable to walk without the aid of his stout stick. He had lost his sense of optimism long ago, yet he retained the fierce independence of the young man who moved to Israel more than three decades ago. His routine, which began at five and ended late into the night, was the price Abraham had to pay to live in the Holy City. In India, he had a life of privilege, education, money and servants. Here, he could not afford to retire or hire help.

It was not that he had not worked hard, nor that he had no family to hand. Abraham had grafted all his life and yet still could not muster enough of a pension to retire. He lived with his second son and family in one of Jerusalem's better suburbs in a modern house with a small garden. From the living room one could see a dramatic panorama of the city. A concrete ring of tower blocks nestled in the hills surrounding the old city, a modern-day fortress to keep out the enemy. Within the next concentric circle lay the newer part of the city, with the emblems of the nation state: opulent hotels, grand museums, government buildings and the Knesset. At the very heart was the eternal city of gold, Old Jerusalem. From a great distance, the pearl-like shimmer of the Western Wall concourse can be visible on a clear day, alongside the

iridescent majesty of the Dome of the Rock. After all the incantations of longing to go to Jerusalem one day, now Abraham could gaze upon it every morning from his window, taking in the millennial sweep of history over a cup of tea. From a distance it seemed perfect, the dream everything he hoped it would be. But as the brutal reality of everyday existence zeroed in, life in the Holy City was one of long working hours, high taxes, a crippling cost of living and fear.

Culturally, it was very different from the Jewish way of life in India. Here, society was fast, modern and westernized, with Israeli society taking many of its cues from the United States. Religion sometimes seemed to take second place to survival in the lives of many ordinary busy Israelis, while lying at the very heart of the country's political troubles.

When Abraham and his family had chosen to make the *aliyah*, they saw it as a spiritual homecoming. The weight of expectation was so great after two thousand years of exile that it was bound to end in anti-climax. He fully expected faith to be at the centre of everything, much as it was in Jew Town in Kerala. There religion permeated every facet of daily life, whether a person was Hindu, Muslim, Christian or Jewish. The village pace of life made it easier to accommodate God and ritual into everyday existence. There life had been financially easier as well. Living in Israel meant having to work longer hours to pay higher bills, which meant that a lot of people could not afford to even respect Sabbath here in the Holy Land.

But most of all, Kerala had afforded him peace of mind.

Co-existence was not an aim for ideal times, but simply the way there. The Jew would invite the Muslim into his home as a trusted friend. The Muslim would bring sweets to the Jew when he broke his fast during Ramadan, sharing his blessings. In Jerusalem, for the first time in his life, Abraham had to rewire this logic and go against his natural instincts to live in a city where a Muslim brother, whether Palestinian or any other nationality, was equated with fear.

I first met Abraham at his office on Hamag Street in central Jerusalem. It was a modern building with an outpatient section in the foyer. An armed security guard, a Somali Jew, manned the entrance and scanned the bodies and bags of all who entered for traces of explosives. He did it as if it were no big deal, rather like asking visitors to put on an ID badge. This was routine procedure in the city which had until recently been targeted by waves of suicide bombers after the beginning of the second intifada.

Abraham's office was at the end of a corridor to the right of the foyer. He stood up to greet me, a dark-skinned man with kindly eyes screened behind thick glasses and the familiar Indian paunch protruding beneath his jumper. A small white knitted *kippah* covered his bald head, framed by a halo of fine silvery hair. He wore a shirt, a thick ribbed brown sweater pulled tight over his belly, and grey slacks. He had a ready smile with neat, even teeth. When he saw that I was an Indian, his face was animated with evident delight.

Abraham spoke in soft, precise cadences, emanating a kindly wisdom like Yoda from Star Wars. He offered a chair

and immediately made arrangements for coffee to be served, diligent in his duties as the host. He seemed particularly concerned I was not taking sugar and personally tore open a sachet and poured its contents into my cup, as if worried that I should miss out on a treat. Seeing I was comfortable, he settled back into the administrative chaos of his small empire. A cassette-player tinkled Bollywood music in the background, the notes of its jangling melodies floating through the open window like pollen into the courtyard garden below.

Every bit of available space on his desk was covered in piles of medical correspondence: claims, follow-up paperwork, sets of accounts, plus great bundles of unopened letters that still had to be sifted and sorted. Abraham sat with his hands folded in his lap, still and calm amid this paper storm. It was a throwback to every Indian office I had ever visited: a mysterious, unfathomable eastern order concealed amidst the disarray of brown files, paperwork and half-eaten pakoras.

He reminded me very much of his first grandchild, Anil, whom I had met in Cochin. Anil clearly held a cherished spot in his grandfather's affections and remained at the forefront of his thoughts and prayers. More than anyone in his family, Abraham worried for his grandson's future and his marriage prospects in particular. It was to become a recurring theme in our conversations: the need for Anil to find a Jewish wife.

He told me his family was from Ernakulam, where he had once managed a construction business. There he had been a wealthy man with land and property and good connections from his days as a senior member of the ruling Communist

party. He dabbled in politics and even considered a political career, but decided to forsake all that for the chance to come to Israel. For his family, Israel was a matter not of choice, but of faith.

But having returned 'home', Abraham found the Jewish observances were often ignored in this modern, secular nation. The pace of life was faster, more expensive, less bound by tradition. In his late seventies, he found himself living the eternal dream in the Holy Land, yet somehow the spiritual moorings of his life had been loosened. Now after thirty years, he was thinking of returning to India.

'After I came here, after six months I saw this place is no good for me, I want to return to Cochin,' he told me, his small head wobbling in anxiety. 'Unfortunately, we sold all the properties there. So many times I tried to go back to Cochin. But I found I could not, for some reason or another. Now on 10 January, I'm going. Not for holiday. Maybe I'll never come back.'

I asked him why he was leaving Jerusalem now, after so much and after so long? The city meant everything to him. It had been worth losing India for thirty years.

'Jerusalem!' He sighed, twiddling the volume control on his tape recorder as he turned up a hit he particularly favoured. 'If you come one time, it *is* paradise. But to stay...' His voice trailed off sadly, cheeks puffed out in dismay like a sad child. 'In Cochin there was no trouble, there was no trouble for Jews. Here, it's a different story. Yesterday, you asked me to meet you there, at your residence.' I was staying at the Notre

Dame guesthouse just outside the old city walls. 'I couldn't come there. We're afraid to come there, near East Jerusalem. They're dragging people, shooting people.'

'You go to the Wailing Wall?' I asked.

'Wailing Wall, I'm going. But I'm taking the bus number two from here and just going to the Wailing Wall. When I'm before the Wall, I feel I'm standing before heaven.' He paused as he briefly journeyed into his memories before coming back to me again. 'Then I return home by bus,' he said. 'The Wall is safe, the bus is safe.'

But Israel generally was not, he believed. I was to find out that Abraham had suffered an internal struggle for some time. On the one hand, in this city he believed he was closer to God. He marvelled that he was lucky enough to be able to visit the Wall albeit not as frequently as he would wish. Whenever he did go, it comforted him and made up for all he had relinquished. He had fulfilled the religious duty to return to the Holy Land. But three decades on, it was not enough. Israel failed to fill the emotional and spiritual vacuum in his heart after he left India. He was saddened to see the lack of religious observance in the Holy Land, he felt neglectful of his own duties as a Jew because he was too busy working and prayed less than he did in Cochin. He saw how modern ways were taking his own family further away from the traditions of the faith that had ruled their lives in Cochin. Last, the political violence corrupted his peace of mind. He was still a man of the village. He remembered how Jew, Muslim and Christian had lived as friends and neighbours and in this new life he

could not reconcile the clash between the ethos of his faith and culture and the political cost of realizing the dream of the Promised Land.

Abraham's eldest son, Sam, father of Anil and Solomon, had also come out to Israel in 1971. Abraham and his wife followed two years later with their parents. Initially, they were all flushed with optimism at the thought of resettling here. With his skills as a manager for a major construction company in Kerala, Abraham felt he had something valuable to contribute to a country which needed to build itself from scratch. The construction dream never materialized. Also, in the end, Sam and his family were defeated by the violence and siege-like atmosphere that was part of Israel.

After Sam's arrival, war broke out in 1973. In October that year Egypt and Syria launched an attack on Israel on the day of Yom Kippur. Sam fought in that war and then again in the 1984 war with Lebanon. He was a tank driver and saw action on the front line. He did not wish to resurrect the experience. The wars marked him deeply. Unlike Bezalel, he could not reconcile himself to the violence which was so against everything he had ever known in India. It helped him to decide to leave and return to Kerala.

'He got a shock from the war,' Abraham explained. 'We all did. My wife became ill and then in 1985 she expired. Sam also suffered deeply from his mother's death and that was it. He decided to go back to Cochin.'

Anil had told me in Cochin that his father rarely spoke of those days of conflict in 1973 and 1984. He felt uneasy

fighting against men who looked much like those he had grown up alongside in India, men who were not so different from old friends. He fulfilled his duty to his country, but he was not a fighting man. He did not want this for his sons, who were still very young, so the family went home. Abraham told me the fear of Israel being destroyed had passed. Yet the internal security menace remained ever present.

'We're still afraid because of the security situation. All the places for Jews have security. Even here you've seen the security guard. In India Jews had a very peaceful existence. In Ernakulam we were surrounded by so many people of different religions. On Jew Street we had one mosque and two synagogues. Yet we saw no trouble with our neighbours.

'Why do I think of going home? I'm an old man. I wish to have peace, to pray in peace. In Cochin there was no tension. No tension,' he emphasized, lifting his hands to the skies and letting them fall again. 'In all the places where we lived – Cochin, Chennamangalam, Parul – no tension.'

Even as he spoke of no tension I could feel his tension. And little wonder. Earlier that year there had been a brief but brutal skirmish. Israel's northern settlements had faced rock-launcher bombardment from Lebanon, incurring an Israeli retaliation with all its formidable firepower. Yet this bloody confrontation, which the world watched in dismay, was less of an immediate concern to Abraham than the ceaseless paranoia of suicide bombings in the city where he lived. This was the 'tension' he spoke of: the crippling dread of an invisible enemy, an enemy who might even look like your

friend, who could blow up a bus, a car or a marketplace at any time.

'For now, Jerusalem's more calm,' he told me. 'But for how long? Before, each month, each week there were explosions of suicide bombs in Jerusalem. Every week. Every week from 2003 to 2005, every week there was news of a suicide bombing. So many Israelis died.'

He compared this with India, where there was no history of Jews being targeted by fanatics. The synagogue was next to the police station in Mattancheri, yet the threat was deemed so minuscule that I rarely saw the police officer awake at his post. There, of course, the situation was very different. The Jews had been such a tiny minority group that they did not register on the political radar of militant religious groups from either Hinduism or Islam. There they were not power brokers. Here, the Kerala Jews had to wake up to a relentless struggle for their survival. After thirty years, Abraham was tired of struggling.

*

The next day was Shabbat, so Abraham would spend his day at the local synagogue. On Sunday he worked as usual until three. He told me that he had not visited the Wall for six months. He was put off by the journey and the security fears, so I offered to pick him up from work and go there with him. He seemed pleased with the suggestion and agreed.

He told me that for all Jews the Wall represented sacrifices.

After the destruction of the Second Temple almost two thousand years before, the only remaining part was the Western Wall. The ancient Jews had sacrificed their lives to protect it. Today it was a place to remember, a place to supplicate before God.

He issued me with instructions ahead of our visit, already excited. 'The first time people visit they feel they can bring their problems here. Even Hillary Clinton came and put her paper in the wall. You can put your request to God in this place and here you will receive the answer.'

I could imagine what Hillary had asked for. Abraham told me I should also write a petition to place in the Wall. He told me the Wall was the only reason he came to Israel. It was the reason he had stayed so long. I asked him if he had ever offered a petition at the Wall. 'Only twice. Both times, He answered,' he replied.

On Sunday afternoon I picked him up in the car. The Palestinian driver Nazeeh decided he would use the journey as an opportunity to ask how he could get a job as an ambulance driver, as tourism earnings had collapsed since the conflict with Lebanon. The two dipped in and out of Hebrew and English. Abraham told Nazeeh that the rules were very strict, that one would need a clean driving licence for at least two years – that meant no tickets, no accidents. This set off the usually mild-mannered Nazeeh. He launched into a tirade about the iniquity of such a requirement. As he turned around to me to protest, paying no attention to the traffic, he shouted: 'It is impossible! Show me a driver in Jerusalem with no tickets

and I show you a man who does not drive. Two years is too long. And you're telling me I must have no accidents in this time? Can you believe this?' He gestured to me in the rear mirror.

'The job's for an ambulance driver. Is it unreasonable to expect a driver who does not cause accidents?' I replied.

'Perhaps.' He shrugged. 'But for Israeli, I am sure there is no problem getting through this paperwork. For Palestinian, always extra demands, bigger headaches. Still, I will try. The old man says what to lose, eh?'

The old Jew and the young Palestinian seemed to get on well. At one stage they became engrossed in an amusing conversation in Hebrew and laughed uproariously. When I asked what they were discussing, Nazeeh looked sheepish and replied untruthfully, 'Don't worry. It's not so interesting.'

We arrived at the entrance by Dung Gate at 3.30 p.m., near the car park. The huge plaza that stands before the vast Western Wall is accessed only through a high-security check-point – an airport-style walk-through screening to detect weapons or explosives, plus a bag check by Israeli officers. Abraham fished into his bag and gave me a cream silk headscarf to cover my head before going to the Wall. The plaza was thronging with people. There were few tourists, but mostly Jewish families.

The Wall towered before us. The vast structure was built of huge pale gold slabs of Jerusalem stone, some of which were two metres high. In its time, the Second Temple had been a vision of God's glory on earth. The walls were adorned

with white marble, delicately veined with lines of red and blue. The ancient Jewish historian Flavius Josephus describes doors of gold leading into the *Hekhal* which were further embellished with 'golden vines from which depended grape clusters as tall as a man'. A curtain of scarlet, blue and purple linen and embroidered with sun, moon and stars hung above the doors.

Josephus described the Temple's supporting walls as 'the greatest ever heard of'. The longest of them was the western wall, which measured 530 yards. The stones used for these walls were massive, with some weighing as much as five tons. The sanctuary of the Temple was gilded and from a distance the building was an ethereal vision of white and gold, dazzling onlookers in the sunlight, as if Yahweh himself had blinded them with his presence for a moment.

Abraham headed towards the men's section of the Wall, while I went to the women's section on the right. The approach was down a steep path that led directly to the bare stone. White plastic chairs were sporadically set out to allow people to sit and pray, contemplate or just rest. Low wooden lecterns stood ready with copies of the Torah.

The women, heads covered by squares of silk, lined up in rows against the Wall, some gently rocking side to side while holding their arms across their chests, others with heads bobbing back and forth, their faces pressed up against the bare stone. Here the Jews come to commune directly with God. Several of the women were weeping, wet cheeks pressed against the pages of the open Torah, forehead and

bodies leaning into the Wall as they sobbed their entreaties into the sun-warmed stone. Tears coursed down the cheeks of many of the women who prayed here, from old orthodox Jews, dressed head to toe in black, with thick dark stockings and sensible shoes, to young mothers rocking their toddlers or swaddled newborn in their arms. There were young female Israeli soldiers, their carelessly slung rifles a striking contrast to their demure and pious demeanour. I watched one beautiful young Jewess, silky black hair swathed in a pink scarf of roses that framed her perfectly made-up face as she bowed her head in prayer, rocking on her black stiletto boots, arms wrapped tight around her white fake-fur jacket.

Young and old, black and white. There was no sound discernible apart from the weeping and murmur of passages of the Torah. Lovebirds, sleek with chests blushing a soft pink, swooped overhead and settled into cracks in the wall high up, watching the people below. Tiny sparrows whizzed above our heads and burrowed into the gaps to feed their chicks. The lower cracks and crevices between the huge slabs of stone were jammed with countless scraps of white paper, each one containing a personal epistle.

Time passed quickly as I sat and watched the tide of people. They shed tears in a way I had rarely seen, even at other significant places of pilgrimage for other faiths. Why did they cry so? Was it for themselves? Was it a sudden realization of the pain suffered by their people over the millennia, or did they cry for the burden of a history which

continued to deny them peace, even here in the Promised Land? The Wall was a place to unload the agonies of past and present, personal and communal.

When a space cleared, I did as Abraham suggested and placed my own petition amidst the thousands of others, as non-Jews are allowed to do. I left to meet up with him. He was slowly making his way across the plaza, a tiny little figure in a green puffa jacket in the midst of this vast sea of white stone.

'What did you pray for?' I asked. 'Did you pray to return to India?'

'Not India. I prayed for Anil. My firstborn grandchild. I pray that he finds a good girl to marry. He desires marriage above all else for his happiness. That is all.'

'You prayed for a Cochini Jewish girl?'

'Not just Cochini. Those days are gone. Any Jewish girl. But she must be soft-minded, a good heart. I only ask God, "Give him a wife who will not give him headache."'

I thought once again of the peppercorn necklace in Anil's pocket. His quest was now in the arena of the highest power.

*

Afterwards, Nazeeh dropped us off at Abraham's house. In the kitchen–living room his fourteen-year-old granddaughter was sprawled on the floor with her friend, television blaring, as they roared with laughter at an Israeli stand-up comedian. She barely acknowledged him as Abraham introduced us and

set about making tea and cutting thick slices of cake. In sharp contrast to the old-fashioned courtesy that the young show the old in India, this young girl ignored her grandfather, turning up the TV to drown his voice. He limped about the kitchen, refusing my offer of help and insisting on acting the host, in the Indian way.

The family chihuahua nipped my shoe and then settled by my feet as I drank tea, eyes like black coals smouldering in the snow of his white fur, as if looking for any sign of provocation to attack. As his granddaughter continued to ignore him, Abraham repeated with quiet emphasis that it was time to leave Jerusalem.

'I see now this isn't for me. My son and grandchildren here are not keeping the Sabbath and festivals. Not because of work, they don't care for our religion. In three decades, I've made the journey from Israel to India nineteen times. I've more feeling for the grandchildren there, you see.'

Abraham was surrounded by family in this house. He couldn't move for family. He worked and lived an active life and he was in the land of his forefathers. He prayed at the Wall, which seemed to be his only source of comfort in a city that was a stranger. In his first winter in Jerusalem he had experienced snowfall. It measured twenty centimetres and he remembered the shock of seeing tiny ice crystals in the shape of flowers. At the time it seemed magical and emblematic of a new life, which seemed to offer every possibility. Now when he thought of snow, there was no glitter of delight in his eyes. The snowfalls in Jerusalem

merely made him recall the warmth of Cochin. The un-observed Sabbath reminded him of prayers in the houses of friends in Ernakulam. The drudgery of his working life here underscored the life of ease he had forsaken. And every time he watched the news to see pictures of carnage and war, he thought of Jew Town, his friends from the synagogue and the mosque and the temple.

'As a young man, when I first came here, I told myself, "Abraham, this is heaven." Now I know. *Not* heaven.' He broke off a piece of cake, offering it to the dog, who licked it up eagerly. Now as he approached his ninth decade, Abraham wanted to overturn his life once more, leave the land of his prophets and make a fresh *aliyah* back to India.

'I am more than seventy. I am in my last years and I think nothing of the future,' he told me, head wobbling gently from side to side, palms resting flat on his thighs. 'I don't worry. I really don't worry any more. I only seek a calm life now, to finish my life with calmness. To die in calmness. In Cochin. This is my wish.'

*

Later that afternoon after leaving Abraham, I walked through Jaffa Gate, one of the vast gateways that lead into the ancient citadel city, and made my way towards the Tower of David. Its pale stonework glowed in the dying sunshine. I bought a ticket and passed through the gates into gardens of blue lavender that filled an old courtyard suffused with its perfume.

I mounted the sequence of steep stairs that led to the viewing platform at the top, which afforded uninterrupted views across the rooftops of Old Jerusalem. The sun was descending and hung low now, a mellow orange disc in pale blue skies. The city lay below, an ancient and intricate labyrinth of gold and shadow that has been the source of such spiritual inspiration and suffering. I could see tiny figures thronging the narrow walkways that threaded together the separate quarters of the city. Each was a microcosm of Jerusalem's heritage, peoples who had loved the city and spilled blood for it over the millennia.

In the middle distance was the Temple Mount, the disputed site which is venerated by both Muslims and Jews, and therein the gold glint of the Dome of the Rock shrine and the silver of El-Aqsa Mosque. The surrounding paths led to the heart of the Arab souk in the Muslim quarter, which was packed with women shopping for provisions, some wearing designer jeans, others cloaked in the anonymity of the burqa with just almond kohl eyes visible, their masked vivaciousness evident in scarlet-painted toenails. They haggled with the stallholders without pity for profit, selecting the choicest produce, beating down the prices, before gathering their brown-paper parcels to their bosom. There were handsome clean-shaven youths and bearded old men with sun-withered faces of parchment, earnest in conversation as they walked in pairs, sometimes hands lightly linked in friendship as is the eastern way. Those on their way to the mosque wore prayer caps as they hurried for *namaaz*, attired in immaculate white robes that somehow

defied the film of dust that engulfed all else. Others dressed in Arab-style headscarves and expensive kaftan robes, their wealth displayed by thick gold rings and bracelets glinting upon fingers and wrists.

Whole lanes were devoted to spices and condiments, others to brass pots and kitchenware. In the food market, hawkers hollered out prices in Arabic, proffering buyers a taste of olives and dates or sugar-dusted Turkish delight shot through with slivers of pistachio or flavoured with essence of lemon and rose. Pomegranates were spliced open to reveal creamy insides studded with seeds as bright as rubies in a Pasha's jewelled turban. In the meat quarter, halal butchers brandished fearsome bloodied choppers that deftly sliced stacks of mutton ribs or quartered chickens beneath the scrutiny of fearsome elderly matriarchs, moustaches bristling at the slightest hint of being cheated.

The Via Dolorosa in the Christian quarter, the path once taken by Christ as he carried his cross to Calvary, is lined now with scores of souvenir shops such as the 'Ninth Station Boutique' which are run by Christian Palestinians. As one traces the steps of Christ on his path of suffering, one is assailed by the sight of thousands of religious icons, gold-leafed halos in resplendent relief. Wall upon wall of crosses, rosaries and scapulas, precious vials of holy water from the river Jordan or earth excavated from Bethlehem and entombed in tiny lockets, promising to ward off manifold evils. Pavement galleries depicting the Crucifixion, the Last Supper, Mary and Baby Jesus, as shopkeepers beckoned

passing trade with open palms and the eastern promise of 'Very cheap' or 'Very antique'.

In the warren of lanes that led to the Jewish quarter and Western Wall, the Jews made their way to the security gates: orthodox Jews who made Jerusalem their mission, wearing wide-brimmed hats and heavy black coats, impervious to the climate; conservative womenfolk in headscarves and wigs grasping the hands of rose-cheeked, *kippah*-capped children. They skipped quickly towards their destination, as if running late for an appointment, watched by Palestinian shopkeepers whose eyes burned with a thousand suppressed grievances.

From high above the old city, the rushing figures seemed one and the same, a blur of flowing robes in the colours of the landscape itself. The tableau seemed set in a time beyond modernity. As the shadows deepened, the fragrance of lavender and incense, shaami kebab and fried onion appeased the senses. In the distance the shimmering white concourse of the Western Wall shone still. And beyond lay the majestic Dome of the Rock, marking the site of a black rock where it is believed Muhammad ascended to heaven on his white steed after completing his Night Journey. The Rock is seen by both Muslim and Jew as 'the centre of the world, the entrance to the Garden of Eden, source of fertility', according to Armstrong's *A History of Jerusalem*. Who holds the key to this sacred gateway remains a source of strife – any threat to this place from one or the other could ignite the whole of Jerusalem once more.

Yet from a distance, all one discerned was beauty and it did not seem possible that stones had the power to make a city bleed. If one sat high above the old city and listened during the course of one day, one could hear the peal of bells from the Christian quarter, the haunting cry of the muezzin from the Muslim quarter and the triumphal blast of the *shofar*. Yet unlike in Kerala, in Jerusalem the sounds spoke of discord not unity.

After dropping Abraham at his house, Nazeeh had told me he appreciated the old man's manners. It was his city too, and yet many Israelis made him feel he did not belong. He had not felt that with the old man. He was all the more approving when he heard of the Jews' relations with the Muslims in India itself. It was all a revelation to him. In this city where his forefathers had grown up, Nazeeh constantly fretted for the future of his children. Would they have the chance of a good job; would they have a house of their own; or the chance of peace? Last and most worrisome of all, would a place remain for them in their ancestral land? He had no answers. Some of these questions had also preoccupied the Cochini Jews and compelled many to leave their interim paradise for Israel.

Here Nazeeh had little optimism for relations between the two warring brothers and pointed to the wall that was being constructed at that time along the West Bank, severing the Palestinian community from their source of work, water supply and the outside world. He believed this effective apartheid was a way of crushing his community's future into the dust.

This was part of the unease that plagued some of the older Cochini Jews who came to Israel. Some, but not all. The issue of division within the Holy Land itself had not been a cause for concern for the Zionists among them. Whenever we discussed the subject of the Arab-Israeli conflict, men like Bezalel and Isaac viewed the battle for survival as necessary, part of a destiny that had been set out for the Israeli people. It was not for them to question.

Yet others, among the Malabari immigrants in particular, sensed an echo of their own tragedy in the Palestinians. They too knew what it was to be usurped in their historical narrative, to face separation. In Kerala, division had led to destruction. Perhaps their fear was of the cycle repeating itself.

This was all part of the 'tension' that Abraham spoke of. His faith was rooted in Judaism as a religion of justice. He remembered that the Jews and Muslims sprang from the same founding father – the Prophet Abraham. Therefore theirs was an unnatural enmity.

After so much anticipation and the divided history of the Black and White Jews in Kerala, Abraham, his son Sam and others like Babu found that the just society they had craved, the shalom that comes from harmony, was absent even in the Holy Land. Sam and Babu's judgement had been swift: Israel was not home.

It had taken Abraham thirty years to make his decision to leave. In the end he was defeated by a spiritual dislocation and insecurity that was too high a price to pay. In the period

that followed my visit, the suicide bombings would worsen, magnifying the nightmare. His imminent return took the saga of the Kerala Jews full circle. It had begun three thousand years ago in the magnificent fortress city that stretched before me. The Temple, that touchstone of faith, was destroyed, and pain resonated to this day in all the Jews who came to the Western Wall. India was meant to be no more than an interim paradise, but more than two thousand years of history had made the Jews as much a part of the fabric of India as the Hindus, Muslims or Christians. After nourishing the dream of Jerusalem for millennia, Abraham's generation finally made the joyous pilgrimage home.

For men like Bezalel, their mission was fulfilled. It was as if they were whole again. In a remarkable reinvention, they relinquished the past, choosing to revive all that was best from India in the motherland. Their homecoming provided renewal at a time when the old life in Cochin was beyond redemption.

Yet Abraham encountered alienation and sorrow. Sixty years have passed since Indian Independence, since the formation of Israel – geopolitical landmarks which ushered in the compulsion for change in the lives of ordinary men and women. After three decades of war and the guerrilla warfare of terrorism and counter-terrorism, Abraham remained unable to reconcile faith with conflict. It was true that it was over for his people in Kerala. Yet he foresaw his own imminent demise and preferred it to be within the embrace of the past. This desire to return provided an

unexpected epitaph, compelling Abraham to find rest in a land that had given the Jews so much, a peace that history has rarely bestowed. In the end it was an age-old tolerance that drew him.

References

Adigal, Ilango, *Shilappadikaram: The Ankle Bracelet*, US, New Directions Publishing Corporation, 1965

Allen, Woody, *Complete Prose*, US, Wings Books, 1991

Armstrong, Karen, *A History of Jerusalem*, UK, HarperCollins, 1996

Benjamin, Joshua M., *The Mystery of Israel's Ten Lost Tribes*, India, Mosaic Books, 1989

Benjamin of Tudela, *The Itinerary of Benjamin of Tudela: Travels in the Middle Ages*, US, Nightingale Resources, 2005

Book of Baruch, 2 Baruch, 10

Buchanan, Claudius, *Christian Researches in Asia*, UK, Cadell & Davies, 1812

Correa, Gaspar, *The Three Voyages of Vasco da Gama and His Viceroyalty*, UK, Hakluyt Society, 1968

Diamond, Jared, *Collapse: How Societies Choose to Fail or Survive*, USA, Viking Penguin, 2005

Gandhi, *Book of Quotations*, India, 1931

Goitein, S. D., *A Mediterranean Society: The Jewish Communities of the World as Portrayed in the Cairo Genizah*, US, University of California Press, 1993

Goldberg, David J. and Rayner, John D., *The Jewish People, Their History and Their Religion*, UK, Viking, 1987

Goldman, Israel M., *The Life and Times of Rabbi David Ibn Abi Zimra*, US, Jewish Theological Seminary of America, 1970

Isaac, I. A., *A Short Account of the Calcutta Jews, with a Sketch of the Bene-Israels, the Cochin Jews, the Chinese Jews and the Black Jews of Abyssinia*, India, 1917

Jewish Agency, *Report on the Jews of Malabar*, Israel, 1948

Jews of Cochin, India, India, Jewish Welfare Association

Johnson, Barbara, *Our Community in Two Worlds: The Cochin Paradesi Jews in India and Israel*, PhD thesis, University of Massachusetts, 1985

Johnson, Barbara, 'The Cochin Jews of Kerala' in *The Jews of India*, ed. Orpa Slapek, Israel, Israel Museum, 2003

Josephus, Flavius, *Antiquities of the Jews*, UK, Echo Library, 2006

Josephus, Flavius, *Jewish War*, UK, Penguin, 1981

Jussay, P. M., *The Jews of Kerala*, India, University of Calicut, 2005

Katz, Nathan and Goldberg, Ellen, *A Jewish King at Shingly*, India, Manohar, 2006

Katz, Nathan and Goldberg, Ellen, *Kashrut, Caste and*

Kabbalah: The Religious Life of the Jews of Cochin, India, Manohar, 2005

Katz, Nathan and Goldberg, Ellen, *The Last Jews of Cochin: Jewish Identity in Hindu India*, US, University of South Carolina Press, 1993

Kushner, Gilbert, *Immigrants from India in Israel*, US, University of Arizona Press, 1973

Lawson, Charles Allen, *British and Native Cochin*, UK, Asian Educational Services, 1861

Loti, Pierre, *India*, London, Asian Educational Services, 1903, reprinted 1995

Mandelbaum, David, *A Case History of Judaism: The Jews of Cochin in India and in Israel*, 1981

Mandelbaum, David, 'Social Stratification among the Jews of Cochin in India and in Israel', *Jewish Journal of Sociology*, 1975

Mandelbaum, David, *Society in India*, US, University of California Press, 1970

Mandelbaum, David, *The Jewish Way of Life in Cochin*, US, Jewish Social Studies, 1939

Manimekalai, Dancer With Magic Bowl, India, second century

Menon, K. P. P., *History of Kerala*, India, 1929; Asian Educational Services, 1982

Narayan, M. G., *Cultural Symbiosis in Kerala*, India, 1972

Panikkar, K. M., *Malabar and the Portuguese*, India, Voice of India, 1997

Pliny the Elder, *Natural History*, UK, Penguin, 1991

Pliny the Elder, *The Periplus of the Erythraean Sea*, UK, Hakluyt Society, 1980

Polo, Marco, *The Travels of Marco Polo*, UK, Wordsworth Editions, 1997

Rabinowitz, Rabbi Louis, *Far East Mission*, Eagle Press, South Africa, 1952

Reinman, Shlomo, '*Masa'oth Shlomo b'Kogin*' in *Mikotsin l'eretz Ysrael*, ed. S. Weil, Israel, 1984

Reinman, Shlomo, *The Travels of Shlomo*, Austria, 1884

Shoskes, Henry, *Your World and Mine*, US, Lipton Publishing Corp, 1952

Slapek, Orpa (ed.), *The Jews of India*, Israel, Israel Museum, 2003

The Chennamangalam Synagogue: A Jewish Community in a Village in Kerala, India, synagogue pamphlet

Whitson, William, *The Works of Flavius Josephus*, Milner & Sowerby, 1860